WHILE I WAS OUT

While I Was Out
Two Years That Changed America: A Peace Corps Memoir

A Peace Corps Writers Book - an imprint of Peace Corps Worldwide

Printed in the United States of America
by Peace Corps Writers of Oakland, California.

For more information, contact peacecorpsworldwide@gmail.com.

Peace Corps Writers and the Peace Corps Writers colophon are trademarks of PeaceCorpsWorldwide.org.

Book design and cover creation by Dania Zafar.

ISBN-13: 978-1-950444-36-6
Library of Congress Control Number: 2022913788

First Peace Corps Writers Edition, July 2022

WHILE I WAS OUT

TWO YEARS THAT CHANGED AMERICA:
A PEACE CORPS MEMOIR

JERRY REDFIELD

A PEACE CORPS WRITERS BOOK

To Ruben Patiño,
and all those who worked together to make their communities
a better place for themselves and future generations.

"The times, they are a changing..."

Bob Dylan

CONTENTS

MAPS

My Vacation Trip

SOUTH AMERICA

ECUADOR

LOJA PROVINCE

INTRODUCTION

THIS IS A WORK OF MY HEART MORE THAN MY MEMORY. IT IS taken from my very detailed journal and from letters sent home to my parents who, I discovered to my amazement after my mother died, had kept them intact for many years.

I chose to write this for several different reasons. First, it is for my daughter, to give her some sense of what her dad "did in the war" (I guess that would be the Cold War.) Second, it was written for family and friends who "knew me when," before I left and when I returned from two years of Peace Corps duty in Ecuador during the years 1963 – 1965. For it is as much about what happened while I was in Ecuador as it is about what happened when I returned home. My premise is that the world changed in a major way while I was out and because of that I, as did many others, had a difficult time adjusting to life back home. It is called "reverse culture shock" and I definitely suffered from that. Another group who may be interested in my story is anyone who follows history and the experiences of members of the Peace Corps. Finally, some of this work may be relevant to fans of history and political science. I maintain that what happened in the world of politics drove the changes I encountered upon my return more than any other factors. That may not be the case, but it is here as a reason for how I felt, my reaction to it, and the resultant trajectory of my life.

My journal is the work of a twenty-two and twenty-three-year-old kid/young man (take your pick.) I used much of that content when writing and this work should be read with that tone in mind. My journal is filled with exclamation points brought on by amazement at so many of the events that happened and the attitudes I encountered. Frustration in other places drove more than a few. My first draft was filled with them, but in a bow to my proofreaders and editors, most were eliminated. As you read, please keep in mind that sense of wonderment and incredulity that I had then and, I hope, is still conveyed without them.

Since I was, and still am, an avid book reader, movie buff and a fan of musicals, you will find multiple references to them and quotes from them. I also use a capital "V" for "Volunteer(s)" when describing or referring to my colleagues to avoid using "Peace Corps Volunteer(s)" at every instance. For two key individuals you will meet in the book, I employed "Engineer" and "*Maestro*" as titles (and out of respect) since I had no record or recollection of their first names. Additionally, you will find some then-current expressions, which by now may seem archaic or, as my wife tells me, arcane.

This work was started eight years ago in 2014, pushed aside for a while and finally finished in a flurry of activity. This flurry was motivated by a stage 4 prostate cancer diagnosis and by the COVID-19 pandemic which, with multiple closings and cancellations of travel plans, gave me all the time I needed to work.

I thank my wife for her encouragement and for enduring the view of my back as I worked at the computer. Any errors or omissions or misstatements of names or places are strictly my own due to about a 55-year lapse from the time of the story to the time of its writing. The time lines of the "...And While I Was Out" portions are taken primarily from internet sources and Wikipedia, The Free Encyclopedia, "1964 and 1965 In the United States."

PEOPLE YOU WILL MEET

Peace Corps Administration

Gene Baird: Ecuador Peace Corps Director

James Watson: Director of School Construction, Ecuador

John Smith: Regional Peace Corps Representative (the "Boss")

Dr. Steve Caplin: Peace Corps Doctor (the "Doc")

Mike Agurrie: Regional Peace Corps Representative (the new "Boss")

Ecuadorian School Construction Program Administration

Justo Andrade: School Construction Coordinator; Area C, Southern Loja

Mario Mena: School Construction Paymaster

Engineer Ruilloba: School Construction Engineer

Major Eucadorian Players

In Cangonama:

Padre Reyes: Priest, School Committee head

Señor Espinosa: Building Committee head, neighbor

Maestro Bautista: Master carpenter

Maestro Panama: Master carpenter

In La Toma:

Padre Arias: Priest, "mover and shaker"

Suco Candela: Restaurateur; President, Catamayo Cultural Center

Maestro Illescas: Master carpenter, foreman of school construction

Tomás Vallejo: Park Project Surveyor

Carlos Carrión: Teacher, friend, and neighbor
Luis Garciá: Teacher, friend, and neighbor
Marlene Bermo: Teacher, friend, and cousin of Carlos Carrión
Ruben Patiño: English student, good friend, and supporter of "the cause"

Peace Corps Volunteers - In Approximate Order of Appearance
Joe Orr: Roommate, co-worker in Cangonamá and Loja
Doug Strauss: Roommate, co-worker in Cangonamá and Loja
Gerry Mussett: Volunteer, Loja and Cuenca; roommate in Loja
Joe Kelly: Volunteer, Loja
Armond Joyce: Heifer Project Volunteer, assigned to the Municipality of Loja
Jim Snyder: Engineer, assigned to the Municipality of Loja
John Mulligan: Engineer, assigned to the Municipality of Loja
Chuck Jennings: Volunteer, Cuenca
Ed Delci: Volunteer, Cuenca
Wally Benson: Volunteer, Zamora; roommate in Loja
George Bennett: Volunteer, Zamora
Noble Wiltshire: Volunteer, Cuenca
Bill White: Agriculturalist, assigned to the Municipality of Loja
Rodger Rupee: Volunteer, Loja; roommate in Loja
John Kostishack: Volunteer, Loja; roommate in Loja
Bill Fuzetti: Volunteer, Loja
Paul Bond: Volunteer, Gonzanamá (one of the "new guys")
Tom Wegs: Volunteer, San Pedro and La Toma (another "new guy")

...and more!

APRENDEMOS ESPAÑOL!

(LET'S LEARN SPANISH!)

VOCABULARY	SOUNDS LIKE	DEFINITION
Cangonamá	Kahn-go-nah-Ma	mountain village in Loja province
Cuenca	Kwen-kah	Ecuadorian city in Andean valley
estanciero	S-tahn-C-err-o	owner of large farm or ranch
Gonzanamá	Gon-zah-nah-Ma	mountain village in Loja province
hacienda	ha-C-en-dah	ranch or farm
junta	whoN-tah	a ruling body as a result of a *coup*
Loja	Low-hah	Ecuadorian city and province
minga	ming-gah	volunteer work group
mixto	mix-toe	a bus/truck combination
Quito	Key-toe	capital city of Ecuador
rurales	ruhr-al-lace	rural police
tienda	tea-N-dah	a store
trago	trah-go	a drink
Zamora	Zah-more-ah	city in the *Oriente* area of Ecuador

PREFACE

Our Peace Corps Jeep arrived at about four in the afternoon in this dusty, Ecuadorian mountain top place named Cangonamá. Located at the end of a long, rutted, winding switchback gravel road, ending about 4,800 feet above sea level, it wasn't much to look at. Other than a brick-and-mortar school building under construction, it appeared to be an assortment of not particularly well-built adobe structures. This was a remote little hamlet of about forty to fifty one and two-story homes and had no visible stores, hotels, nor "room to rent" signs anywhere. There was very little stucco or even whitewash on the sides of the adobe homes. If there was ever any such decoration, it had deteriorated long ago. Tile porch roofs were held up by rickety poles. What appeared to be an open sewer was running down the middle of the main pathway through and out of town. No real streets. No street lights nor illumination other than a rather large light on the side of the church where we were to meet our hosts. Today, the sun was quickly beginning to slide behind the mountain top making the place seem even more dreary.

We had been through a lot of training in the U. S. and shuttled from place to place in Ecuador in a fairly structured manner while trying to determine our final assignments. This place was our assignment. Our in-country experiences in Ecuador to date had been in fairly large cities: Quito, Cuenca, and Loja. Now we were on our own. Three guys in the middle of nowhere. What came to my mind was the saying, "This wasn't the end of the world, but you could see it from here." Later that night, as I watched the tail lights of the old Peace Corps Jeep disappear down the rutted road that had brought us into Cangonamá, the thought occurred to me, "We could die up here and no one would ever know."

The "we" in this case were Joe Orr, Doug Strauss and myself. We were three Peace Corps Volunteers who had just come to the end of what had been a grueling four months preparation designed to provide what was called "mid-level technical assistance" to rural Ecuadorian towns and villages involved in the construction of elementary schools. The effort was a part of a United States Agency for International Development (USAID) program under the Alliance for Progress.

Joe, twenty-two years old, with curly blond hair and glasses, hailed from Salt Lake City, Utah. He had received a B.A. from Michigan State University where he made the Dean's List. His background included summer experience as a surveying aide for the U. S. Bureau of Reclamation and a stint as a physical science aide for the U. S. Bureau of Public Health. Joe was smart, quick witted and an astute student of politics, willing and eager to let you know his opinion on any issue of the day. As were many other Volunteers, Joe was a Liberal Arts major with strong interest in political action, best evidenced by his membership in SANE (the National Committee for a Sane Nuclear Policy), an organization working at the time for nuclear disarmament.

Doug, also twenty-two, was tall and thin with dark hair, a thick bushy set of eyebrows and a distinct New York accent which he came by honestly. He grew up on the streets of New York, New York, and was a graduate of Fordham College where he received his A.B. in Inter-American Relations with a minor in Philosophy. Doug at least brought some experience to our project, having done social work and construction in Mexico during the summer of 1962 through a volunteer social work project. His background also included eight months of study in Chile where he acquired some distinctively Chilean accents to his fluent Spanish. Our instructors had tried valiantly, but unsuccessfully, to beat it out of him during our training. As a result, for example, his attempts at saying "Now I am going..." which should have come out as *"Yo, ya me voy..."* came out sounding like, *"Joe, dja mevoy..."* Add a slight New York inflection to the delivery and you get some sense of our instructors' frustration. Joe and I were glad to have him in the mix, as he was the most fluent of the three of us, Chilean accent or not.

The Alliance for Progress, or the *Alianza para el Progreso* was a program launched by the Kennedy Administration to encourage self-determination and cooperation between the U. S., Latin American governments, and the local communities. The role of the local community was to provide voluntary labor, materials and support for the projects involved. In Ecuador this voluntary labor force to perform work for communal benefit was called a *minga*. And that's where the Peace Corps Volunteer came in. Helping form the *mingas* to advance the school construction and other community development projects "to be determined" was part of our mission. Unfortunately, nobody in this remote little town high in the mountain seemed to know anything about us, our arrival, nor our mission.

When we arrived, our welcome was less than enthusiastically overwhelming...to put it mildly. The usual level of Ecuadorian communication on this project had apparently taken place. We were to learn a lot more about this problem in the succeeding months. The local priest, Padre Reyes, and the school committee members had been informed that three new "workers" assigned to the school project would be arriving. Since day laborers (*peónes*) in Ecuador are somewhere on the low end of the social scale right up there (or down there) with ditch diggers, nobody had thought to do anything about arranging lodging for us. So, Padre Reyes, after greeting us, quickly asked his housekeeper, Fidelina, to prepare a meal for the five of us. The two others were John Smith, the Regional Peace Corps Representative who had driven us here, and Dr. Steve Caplin, the newly arrived Peace Corps doctor assigned to monitor and support the health of the Peace Corp Volunteers in all of Ecuador.

The doctor was an interesting character. My guess is he was in his late thirties. Thin, bespectacled and about six feet two inches tall. He had dark hair that had thinned and receded to about the middle of his head, and he had adopted a less than successful comb over to cover it. Dr. Caplin had a sort of nervous energy about him, and he seemed the embodiment of the absent-minded professor type and, for the moment, in awe of his surroundings. His absent mindedness became legendary, and Volunteers were later cautioned not to ride with him if he was behind the wheel.

John Smith was a no-nonsense, forty-five to fiftyish man's man kind of guy. He was a World War II vet with a tanned and somewhat wrinkled complexion that reflected his many years of work in the outdoors. Smith had a sort of an Ernest Hemingway look about him with his big shock of dark hair and a full mustache. He had little tolerance for complaints and was quick to resolve issues for those who had them. Completing the mission was his goal.

Doc Caplin was on an orientation tour. Both Smith and Caplin were headed for Cuenca, more than a day's drive north, at minimum, from where we were located in the southern province of Loja. Having driven six hours from Loja to get us here, they were eager to leave but wanted to make sure that all was well with their charges. To bide time, the Padre agreed to take us on a tour of the town and school construction site and quietly, I suspect, to send out the word for someone to find someplace that would accommodate these three gringos for the foreseeable future. Given what I had seen of the town, what that would look like was anybody's guess.

After a quick tour of the work site, where we discovered the workers had left for the day, we met the local *rurale*, a rural policeman assigned by the Provincial government as the keeper of the peace. It was nice to know there was at least some hint of law and order in the place.

We headed back to the church and Padre Reyes' lodging that adjoined it. He was an affable individual and a good host. A little grizzled, he sported a beret and wore the long traditional black cassock that most priests in Ecuador wear. The Padre was making the best of an uncomfortable situation. He explained to us that our accommodations would not be ready until tomorrow, but that we were free to spend the night in the narthex of the church.

We tried to get our Coleman lanterns going, but to no avail. So much for Yankee ingenuity. The good Padre lent us one of his kerosene lanterns for the evening. He explained that there was also a conveniently located toilet a short walk outside of the narthex that actually had water. An outhouse with a flushable toilet was apparently one of the perks of the priesthood here on top of the mountain. We later discovered that this was the only one in town.

As we sat down for dinner, we were presented with what we were learning was a pretty traditional meal of rice, fried bananas, a squash of some sort on top of greens, and some kind of mystery meat which I suspected was either goat or very tough pork. Doc

Caplin was chattering away in his fractured Spanish, smiling like the Cheshire cat and bobbing his head as if he were the original incarnation of the bobble head dolls. His Spanish was made even more amusing with it being tinged by a strong New York accent which made Doug's sound almost Midwestern. Nervously trying to avoid eating anything that had been touched by water, he enthusiastically praised the food that he was doing a very good job of *not* eating. The Area Representative Smith, on the other hand, had spent plenty of time in the country, as well as time in the Pacific War during the World War II, and appeared to be having no trouble with the conversation nor chowing down on the food. Avoiding the water was something that had been drilled into all of us during our training. We were all equipped with our iodine pills and had been instructed to boil our water as a means of killing off any of the "bugs" that would cause us problems. That was of little help at someone else's dinner table, and we had no way of knowing what things had been washed, nor could we do anything about it if we did. I had successfully avoided "Atahualpa's Revenge," as we called it, during the two weeks in the country that it had taken us to get here, but I now feared this meal might be putting that successful run to an end.

As we were finishing the meal, someone arrived and informed the Padre that a nice two room, upstairs apartment had been found and was being readied for our occupancy in the morning. With that good news John and the Doc made their appropriate farewells, headed out, and I watched those taillights disappear. We chatted a bit more, the Padre said goodnight, and the three of us settled into the pews of the narthex, welcoming the chance to get a good night's sleep at the end of what had been a long, long day.

Somewhere in the night, as I tossed and turned and made an attempt to get as comfortable as I could, the stomach rumbling started. Then the gas. Then the pressure. The need to do the

40-yard dash to the outhouse was upon me. I got up, pulled on my jeans and took off as fast as I could, out the door into the backyard heading for the john. But nobody had told us about the very large dog that the Padre owned. His very own night watchman came at me growling and snarling as I dashed inside the outhouse and slammed the door just in time to avoid his teeth. Ignoring his howling and barking I successfully accomplished my mission. But now I had to deal with "re-entry." Thankfully, a lantern light illuminated the area and I heard the Padre say, "*Señor*, mister? Are you okay?" I said I was, and after he called off the dog and corralled him, I sheepishly thanked him and headed back to the church and my sleeping bag. My now very-much-awake companions gave me no solace but rather a good razzing about my problem. With the assistance of a stomach calming pill and a few more "dog free" trips to the outhouse, (do I call it "silent running?") I was finally able to get to sleep.

That sleep, whatever length it lasted, was broken by a loud commotion outside. "*Ayi, dios mio!*" I heard. Someone had come down to get the priest and let him know that the *rurale,* the local policeman we had met earlier, had been shot while sitting in what passed for a bar in one of the little shacks up the hill. He was still alive, they said, but there being no motorized transportation whatsoever available, he was being placed on a makeshift stretcher and would be dragged down the mountain by a donkey. With that hubbub finally settled, and with the not so comforting thought of what might happen to <u>us</u> in the event of an emergency up here, we again snuffed out the lantern and tried to get some sleep with what was left of the night. "*Bien venido a Cangonamá*!" (Welcome to Cangonamá!) I thought to myself and again pictured those taillights heading down the mountain.

I woke up the next morning wondering, "How did I get myself into this?"

PART I

"ASK NOT...."

HOW DID I GET MYSELF INTO THIS? IT'S A LONG STORY, BUT SOME background on my life and the times we lived in might shed some light on it. Like many others who had joined the Peace Corps, I was a child of the 1950s, the Eisenhower era. I grew up in Pewaukee, a small Wisconsin town twenty miles west of Milwaukee. Now a city, and considered by some a suburb of Milwaukee, it was then a small village surrounded by farmland. Small town values of community, responsibility, patriotism, faith and respect for the law were instilled at home, in school and church. It was a time now seen as idyllic by many. Although we didn't know it then, it was idyllic compared with what was to come in the turbulent '60s. For, as Bob Dylan wrote in October of 1963, *The Times They are A Changing*. And, indeed they were.

In the late '50s and early '60s, Civil Rights legislation and battles over desegregation in schools and the workplace were regularly in the news. The marches and riots were being beamed into America's homes on television showing the brutality and unrest it was causing. Civil rights groups' passive resistance was being met with hatred and brutality. The start of the sexual revolution was underway. "The Pill," approved for contraceptive use in 1960, was changing sexual mores on campuses and in the bedroom. Women were becoming more assertive about their rights and roles in the workplace, but it was still very much a "man's world." Politically, the Cold War was raging. In 1961 the Berlin Wall went up. Following the Cuban Revolution in 1959, Cuba and the Soviet Union were doing all they could in the early 60's to aid and abet the spread of Communist governments in Central and South America. The same was true in African countries where the drives for independence from British and French rule were being infiltrated and influenced by Soviet economic and political inroads.

In 1958, Vice President Nixon had been accosted by angry mobs in Peru and Ecuador. They detested the U. S. policy of giving military aid to support coups in Central America. In Venezuela his motorcade was attacked by hundreds of angry protesters who spat on the cars, smashed the windows, and rocked the president's car until the Venezuelan military were called in to escort his group to safety. The abortive Cuban Bay of Pigs invasion had left a bad taste in the mouths of many Latin American people who looked upon the U. S. as the "Big Bully to the North," interested only in supporting dictators rather than backing them in what was called "the revolution of rising expectations."

Books such as The Quiet American and The Ugly American, published in 1958 (negatively, but accurately) described American activities in Southeast Asia. They gave a prescient view of events that were to take place "while I was out." The Quiet American, considered by some to be anti-American, tells the story of a naïve but well-intentioned CIA agent involved in counter insurgency activities during Vietnam's struggle to free themselves from French rule. The Ugly American describes the United States' losing struggle against Communism in what came to be called the "battle for the hearts and minds of the people" in a fictitious

Southeast Asian country. According to the book, the cause of that loss was due to the Americans' innate arrogance and failure to understand the local culture. In the novel, a Burmese journalist is quoted as saying, "*For some reason the [American] people I meet in my country are not the same as the ones I knew in the United States. A mysterious change seems to come across Americans when they go into a foreign country. They isolate themselves socially. They live pretentiously. They're loud and ostentatious.*" The title of the book is misleading. In common understanding, the "ugly American" has come to mean a loud and ostentatious isolated tourist, traveler or congressman who takes no time to learn the language, customs or culture of the country they visit. The "hero" of the book, Homer Akins, the not so very "ugly American," is portrayed as an engineer who does just the opposite. He lives with the people, comes to understand their needs, and offers genuinely useful assistance by doing small scale projects such as designing and building a bicycle driven water pump. The book argues that the Communists are successful because they practiced tactics similar to those of Atkins. John F. Kennedy was so taken by the book he sent a copy to every U. S. senator because he thought its message so important. Atkins' style is thought by many to be the model for the Peace Corps Volunteers' approach to getting things done in a "can do," people-to-people manner without the need for major and expensive American aid and bureaucracy: learn the language, learn the customs, work face to face, share your knowledge. I had read that book with great interest while in college.

On October 22, 1962, three days before my 21st birthday, the Cuban Missile Crisis had come to a head. President Kennedy came on TV and announced that the U. S. had discovered Soviet made and manned missiles on the mainland of Cuba, ninety miles from our shores. He demanded they be dismantled and removed. Furthering the tension, he announced the blockade of Soviet ships headed for Cuba with even more ordinance. The U. S. and the Soviet Union were in a stand-off over the removal of the missiles, and both countries were looking down the barrels of fully-loaded "nuclear guns." Fortunately, President Khrushchev agreed to remove the missiles in exchange for a promise from Kennedy not to invade Cuba and, secretly, for the U. S. to also remove offensive missiles from Turkey. This diplomacy avoided what could have been a nuclear confrontation that would have killed tens of millions in both countries; both had been ready to go to war. These were the "Happy Days" of the early 1960's.

It was in this environment that I had to make some decisions. That October of 1962, I was a senior at the University of Wisconsin majoring in political science with an emphasis on Latin American Studies. I had about three years of Spanish, a year of French, and a one-year study of Portuguese under my belt...and I had absolutely no idea of what I was going to do upon graduation. Available jobs for Liberal Arts majors as full of themselves as I (now admittedly) was, were in short supply. Selling soap for Procter & Gamble didn't hold a lot of appeal. I was dating a girl named Ann, who had some pretty strong designs on me and my future, but I wasn't eager to commit at that point. My love life while at school had been intense, but sporadic. A few "on again-off again" relationships had left some bad feelings in a number of hearts, including my own.

As spring turned toward summer and graduation day was fast approaching, my angst and discontent increased. All of my fraternity brothers with "real" majors like business, accounting and engineering were busily interviewing or applying for grad school or law school. Some were even planning on getting married. Here was I, a small-town boy, a well-intentioned political science major with some vague long-term political, foreign service or, perhaps, ministerial aspirations who knew a little about Latin America and spoke Spanish *un poco*. Through what I had learned from my faith and education, I knew I wanted to change the world I had been reading about and leave it a better place. I wanted to let citizens of other countries know that Americans were not all bad folk. We were being misrepresented around the world by bad press, our political enemies, and generally screwed up people.

And then I remembered Kennedy's "Ask not" speech at his inauguration: *"Ask not what your country can do for you – ask what you can do for your country."* Some students I knew had applied to the Peace Corps, but they were stuck in limbo awaiting word while interviewing for jobs. The companies were letting applicants know their decisions faster than the Peace Corps bureaucracy allowed. The Corps was losing some good candidates. Then what should appear in the campus newspaper, *The Daily Cardinal,* but an ad with an application for the Peace Corps promising a two-week response time. *"Name your country and we'll let you know."* it said. *"We'll do everything we can to get you your first choice and let you know in two weeks."* This appealed to me and drove my decision to apply.

I thought about all the countries I had studied and would most like to actually visit in Latin America. I chose Costa Rica, a nice little country in Central America with a long history of democratic rule. It was not too far away, had a beautiful mix of terrain, was famous for carts with very pretty wheels, and I could hit both the Atlantic and Pacific Coasts while there. The Peace Corps was good to their word. They let me know in two weeks. I got Ecuador.

CAN YOU SAY "*MARTILLO*"?

WHILE I WAS NOT THRILLED AT FAILING TO GET MY FIRST CHOICE, I was glad to have an assigned country and an assigned project. I was to be part of Ecuador V, the fifth group to go to Ecuador and whose assignment was to help facilitate the construction of schools. The extent of my construction abilities up to that point had been limited to the construction of a bird house for a 4-H project. As I remember, in my frustration to get the corners to align properly, I resorted to pounding the thing with a hammer (in Spanish *martillo*) succeeding only in splitting the roof in two. This, in turn, resulted in a few expletives and my throwing the whole works to the floor. With the help of my dad and a little (lot of) wood filler, I was able to reassemble the whole thing and gingerly cart it off to a meeting where I arrived just in time for it to be presented for evaluation.

So, when people would ask me, "What are you going to do after graduation?" I could now proudly say, "Oh, I'm going into the Peace Corps." And generally, they would smile and say, "Oh that's really neat. Where will you be going?" "Ecuador," I would say, and see this glassy look come into their eyes. "Where's that?" they would ask. And I would say, "South America." "Oh, yeah. Hot down there. What are you going to be doing?" "School construction." "Oh, you an engineer?" was the usual comeback. And I would respond with something like, "Well no, but we'll be doing community development as well." And with that vague description, the conversation usually ended with something like, "Well that's a wonderful thing you're doing, I don't think I'd ever be able to do that." Quite frankly, I wasn't sure if I would be able to do it either. But I would soon find out, first, what community development was and second, if I could do it. The answer lay at the Peace Corps training facility at the University of New Mexico in Albuquerque.

We started training in the heat of July where we, to our great pleasure, learned we were to be joined by a group of female Volunteers heading for health care assignments in Columbia. Among that group of Volunteers was Ann Carlisle, the girl I thought at one point, I might be "leaving behind" at the University. She had suddenly taken a great and patriotic interest in serving her country by signing up for the Peace Corps as well. She had been accepted, and we would be training on the same campus. These health Volunteers would later practice their injection techniques on oranges and then on us.

I can do no better in capturing the essence of the Peace Corps training than to use the words of another Peace Corps Volunteer, Moritz Thomson, in his delightful book about his experiences in Ecuador, Living Poor, A Peace Corps Chronicle:

> Peace Corps training is like no other training in the world, having something in common with college life, officer's training, Marine basic training, and a ninety-day jail sentence. What makes it paradoxical is that everything is voluntary; the schedule exists for you to follow if you wish...Our schedule began at 5:45 each morning and lasted until 9:30 at night. It was a fantastic schedule - what they called a 'structured

> program'- and after the first three days we realized that it was planned that way on purpose. If there were any psychotics who had sneaked through the Washington screening and the Treasury Department investigation (and there were a couple), the Peace Corps wanted to find out fast, and if we were breakable, they wanted to break us in the United States.

"Deselection" was the phrase they used. In addition to teaching the language, history, customs, culture and a modicum of construction skills, that's what the training was all about. You had been "selected in" to the Peace Corps and you did your training under the constant threat of being "selected out."

To again use Thomson's words,

> The purpose of the program was not to change your character but to discover it, not to toughen you up or to implant proper motivations for Peace Corps service but to find out what your motivations were...The training was designed not only to reveal you to the Peace Corps but to reveal you to yourself. At any of the three deselection days [once per month], therefore, while the majority of those deselected felt the most terrible and guilty sense of failure...a few felt relief.

The days started with calisthenics at about 6:00, and we learned to play *futbol,* the now much more familiar sport of soccer and the national sport of all Latin American countries. We learned new respect for those who played it and the stamina it required. Next came breakfast and then classes. Speaking in Spanish was required at all times, halting and mangled though it was for most. We did rope courses in the park; we climbed sheer cliffs; we rappelled; we hiked miles in the mountains; we slept in bed rolls in the rain; and we learned how to make chisels in blacksmith shop. All skills we would probably never use and all done under the watchful eyes of the psychologists with their little clipboards. The psychologists wrote reports; the instructors filled out their evaluations; and all this ended up with the chief Peace Corps psychologist, who after reviewing it all, determined whether or not one was to take the "next step."

After over two months of formal training, our group of men and the companion group of women training for health care assignments in Columbia headed off to Taos, New Mexico, for community development projects there and in the surrounding smaller towns. This was long before Taos was the very popular ski resort destination it is today. It was still a sleepy little town with many dusty streets. One of my group's projects was to assemble and install wooden street signs on the corners of those streets. The other was to socialize with the opposite sex after long days in the hot sun. But that's another story all together. Suffice it to say (for now) that this socialization led to Volunteers making a number of trips between Ecuador and Columbia in the subsequent two years. Several marriages resulted after that.

We did our project assignments in small groups. Our street sign project was good duty compared to some of the others. The purpose of these projects was the "final filter" in the evaluation process and, thankfully, I passed it successfully. Some did not. We returned to Albuquerque to hear the news, to get our "marching orders," to have a brief leave, and to receive instructions on how and where to assemble for the men's flights to Ecuador and the women's to Columbia.

One person, who on doctor's orders, would not be making the journey was my girlfriend Ann. Prior to coming down for training she was involved in a train wreck between Milwaukee and Chicago that had damaged her back. She had sat out most of the physical activities required for her group, and the doctors felt she should not be risking the prospects for further damaging it in an assignment in a foreign country.

While we did not have a lot of time together during training due to the scheduling, we had taken every opportunity to get together when we could, and our romance had intensified. During our leave we spent some time together at the Indiana Dunes State Park on the shores of Lake Michigan about an hour and half from Ann's home, where I managed to sunburn my legs and ankles to a crisp. Soon after that, my mother and dad came down to Arlington Heights, Illinois, where Ann's mom and family gave me a great send-off party ending with tearful goodbyes and promises to write. The next day I flew from O'Hare to New York where I was to catch the plane to Ecuador.

...AND WHILE I WAS <u>NOT</u> OUT

Spring and Summer, 1963

As I mentioned in the introduction, my premise is that the United States went through fundamental changes "while I was out" in Ecuador. Those changes involved the nature of politics; the impact of the Civil Rights legislation; the heating up of the Vietnam War and the resistance to it; the Cold War; the Space Race; and major changes in culture including technology, mass marketing, music and entertainment.

While I was busy getting ready to take finals and preparing for graduation, the spring of 1963 was filled with a number of events that were soon to change the face of the America in which I had grown up. And as we began our 6:00 a.m. to 9:00 p.m. training that summer, the world outside went on with significant events as well. Although we were not unaware of them, our concentration was on ourselves and "making it through." Significant happenings that would soon erupt into bigger issues included:

Politics:

- President Kennedy signs the Equal Pay Act of 1963 and announces his intention to pass a Civil Rights Act.
- In the case of *School District of Abington Township v. Schempp,* the Supreme Court rules that mandated Bible reading or prayer in schools is unconstitutional.

Civil Rights:

- Police dogs and fire hoses are used against demonstrators in civil rights protests in Birmingham, Alabama, led by Ralph Abernathy and Rev. Martin Luther King Jr.
- Civil rights protesters in Washington D. C., and Cambridge, Maryland, are confronted by National Guardsmen.
- Governor George Wallace stands in the doors of the University of Alabama to prevent the entry of African American students as they are escorted to their classes by 100 National Guardsmen as President Kennedy ordered.
- Medgar Evers, the Mississippi State Field Secretary for the NAACP and a WWII veteran is murdered by a White Citizens Council member.
- Six nights of disturbances and unrest follow the burning of crosses in front of the Chicago home of an African American family that had moved into a previously all white neighborhood.
- Martin Luther King Jr. delivers his "I Have a Dream" speech at the March on Washington (where Joan Baez and Bob Dylan also participate.)
- The 16th Street Baptist Church in Birmingham, Alabama, is bombed by KKK members killing four girls and injuring 22 others.

Vietnam:

- The Viet Cong guerillas in the Mekong Delta are being monitored by U. S. troops in helicopters. (By the end of 1963 there would be 16,000 U.S. troops in Vietnam.)

Space:

- In Russia, the first woman, Valentina Tereshkova goes into space.

International:

- President Arosemena of Ecuador is overthrown and exiled by a four-man military *junta* and The Communist Party of Ecuador is outlawed.

Culture:

- Tab, the first diet drink from a major company, is introduced.
- The first push button phone is introduced.
- Zip codes are introduced.

QUO VADIS?

OUR GROUP FROM ECUADOR V MET AT IDLEWILD AIRPORT ON Thursday night, October 24, 1963. (The airport would soon become known as John F. Kennedy Airport, but we didn't know it at the time.) The next day was my 22nd birthday, and I would celebrate its arrival in the air. While waiting to leave, we all stood around, a little nervous, a little tired, anxious to get going and yet apprehensive as well. Was this the right thing to be doing? Were we ready? We all knew we were going to Ecuador, but where exactly? We didn't know.

A few guys from the New York area who had been deselected came to see us off. They had either been appealing their cases or trying to find jobs but were eager to wish us well. We had a few drinks at the bar, swapped lies, told some sick jokes, reminisced about the girls we had left or were leaving behind and then boarded the four-engine prop plane at 11:00 p.m. - the first step of a big experience.

Miami came and went. Kiss the U. S. A. goodbye, boys. Seven hours later, the morning of my 22nd birthday, we stopped and refueled in Tocumen, Panama. Then off to Cali, Columbia, and a delay for engine trouble, and finally a short hop into Quito, the capital of Ecuador, which is nestled in the Andes Mountain range. As we arrived, I looked out the windows of both sides of the plane and saw only mountains. I hoped there wasn't one in front as well.

After our 14-hour journey we landed and were met by a number of Peace Corps personnel and the Consul (vice ambassador) from the U. S. Embassy. The Consul was effusive in his praise and told us how happy he was that we were there and how the people would love us, etc., etc., etc. The group was tired from the flight and just wanted to get some rest. We inquired if he knew anything about where we might end up in Ecuador. He didn't have a clue.

We went to our hotel, the Residencia Lutetia, where I was paired up with Joe Orr for the first time. I had gotten to know him fairly well in training and had even requested him as a possible partner when we were asked who, if we had our preference, we would like to work with on assignment. We discovered we had pledged the same fraternity, Phi Gamma Delta, and went through hell week at our respective universities. But he had decided that fraternity life was not for him and dropped out. We sacked out until about 7:00 and then went down to our first dinner in the country. There was plenty of pork, rice, potatoes, fried bananas and a tomato. We would see a lot more of fried bananas (and rice...and potatoes...and pork) in the weeks and months to come.

The weekend was to be a country orientation at the Peace Corps offices. We hoped we would get some specific information on where we would be going. We met with Gene Baird, the Ecuador Peace Corps Director; and Doctors Monroe and Caplin, who gave us some tips on staying healthy in remote areas. My first impression of Gene Baird was that he was a little nervous and a pretty hardnosed type. Dr. Monroe appeared to be a "cool head" and, as my journal noted, Dr. Caplin seemed "very queer" (in that day's vernacular, very odd.) We asked if they knew where we would be going. They didn't.

On Sunday, we met again at Baird's residence where we met his staff, some Volunteers from the Heifer International Project, and the heads of our school construction projects for the whole country. We asked if they knew where we would be going. They didn't.

Monday and Tuesday brought more orientation meetings and a talk by one of the USAID bosses under whose agency the school construction project was housed. He impressed most of us as the last (we hoped) of the truly <u>ugly</u> Americans. He told us we were involved in "counter insurgency" and were the tip of the spear against communism, etc., etc. (The four-man military *junta* had outlawed the Communist Party of Ecuador in July and had suspended constitutional law.) Whether he was right or wrong, this was not exactly what we envisioned ourselves to be, and he was viewed by most of us as a well-intentioned but dangerous bull in a China shop.

As a result of these meetings, we <u>did</u> at least find out that we were to be split up into three zones in the country: The Coastal Region, the Central Andes Mountain Region, and the Southern Region. A few Volunteers would also be going to the *Oriente* or Amazonian area of the country. The zones were designated as A, B, & C and the Ecuadorian Peace Corps staff leaders of A and B gave their talks and filled the guys in on their areas, what they would be doing and what to watch out for.

Joe and I learned that we would be partners in the Cuenca area about half way down the country from Quito. Cuenca was the headquarters for Area C, the Southern Region. The Ecuadorian leader of the school construction effort in that area was Justo Andrade. Unfortunately, he was not available for comment as he had to officiate at some school dedications. While we had some clue as to the area we would be in, we <u>still</u> had no idea where we would end up. We had to wait until we had <u>another</u> orientation.

After five days in the country, Joe and I, along with the other Area C volunteers, left Quito at 5:00 a.m. on the 290 mile, 14-hour bus ride through the mountains of Ecuador headed for Cuenca. This trip was made even longer due to the military checkpoints that had been established at the entrance and exit of every town of any size ever since the *junta* took over in July.

We were to stay in the Hotel Paris in Cuenca. It should have been named the Hotel *Pulga,* Spanish for "flea." The group went to the orientation meeting the next day scratching and itching and asking for more cans of flea powder for the trip ahead. The meeting was in John Smith's office and was very brief. He said Joe and I would be in the Loja area, another 125 miles to the south. We would be going to Cangonamá, but he didn't know anything about the town. We would have to wait for the orientation in Loja. Smith said we would have to skip the festival scheduled that weekend in Cuenca so that we could go and "get to know Loja." Tired, but happy to know at last where we would end up even though we knew nothing about it, we took a brief tour of the absolutely beautiful city of Cuenca. (Today it is a jewel of a city, home to many ex-pats and now "only" about an eight-hour drive from Quito.)

On Friday, November 1st, we took the 125-mile bus trip further south to Loja. The buses, if one was fortunate enough to get a "high end" one, were little more than school buses with cages on top for luggage. Most buses, on the other hand, were wooden framed, open windowed concoctions built on old truck or bus frames and usually had wooden bench seats. They were dirty, dusty creaky old rigs, and most retained the odor of the chickens or other livestock that passengers often brought aboard. Many were bus-in-front and truck-in-back combinations called "*mixtos*" that we would learn much more about as time went on.

Fortunately, I traveled this route in "high style" with other Volunteers headed for the Loja area: Gerry Mussett, Carmelo Cruz, Joe Kelly, and John Kostishack. We were also accompanied on this trip by a delightful fellow named Armond Joyce, a Volunteer who had been in the country for a while working with the Heifer International Project that introduced healthy, productive livestock into the countryside and taught the locals about their proper care and feeding. Armond would turn out to be a major help in some of my future endeavors.

At every stop along the way we were ambushed by swarms of little urchins as we descended from the bus. Looking for tips, they would come tugging at our legs, saying, "*Meester, le llevo?*" (Mister, can I carry your bags? literally "I'll take you.") We soon became accustomed to this irritant and learned to ignore it, unless feeling particularly sympathetic and generous.

We all checked in at the Crystal Hotel which seemed like a virtual palace after the Hotel Paris/*Pulga*. The problem was that we either brought the fleas with us or in our luggage and now <u>we</u> were the problem. My legs and ankles were covered with bites, and I was apparently allergic to them so they were driving me crazy. Between the sunburn from the Indiana Dunes and the scratching of the bites, I was running out of skin and miserable as hell.

Armond introduced us to some of the local "old timers," Volunteers from earlier groups who were about to finish up their stints or had a year or less to serve. Among these was Barbara Fredrick, from Rhinelander, Wisconsin, who just happened to know one of my college roommates, Roger Boettcher. (Rhinelander was also my father's hometown, and we still had a family cottage on North Pelican Lake.) Small world! Her co-worker was Rosie Schmidt, a cool-headed and very pleasant young woman who, it seemed, was not too happy with John Smith. It appeared that feeling went both ways as John was about to remove them from their assignment.

On Saturday, while taking the two hours necessary to "get to know Loja," we ran into another veteran Volunteer named Robin. He was also from Wisconsin, this time Milwaukee. Robin was bitter as hell about the town, the people, the whole works. He felt he hadn't really gotten too much done and that it was difficult to get anything from the Peace Corps offices. Robin informed us that Smith was hard to work for or with. His advice to us was to "bypass Smith and go to Baird, and then don't expect much."

With that happy bit of information under our belts, we hung around Loja for a few days awaiting the arrival of the much-maligned John Smith to take us out to our work site. We continued to "get to know Loja" for the next six days. That meant mostly eating, drinking and complaining about the lack of organization and lack of action. It was then we learned that Doug would also be going to our same site. At long last, after two weeks in the country, Doug, Joe, John Smith, Doc Caplin and I squeezed into the Peace Corps Jeep for the six-hour ride, out to and up, and up and up to Cangonamá, on some of the scariest, steepest, narrowest, winding and rutted roads I had ever seen.

PART II

SETTLING IN

FOLLOWING THAT FIRST UNSETTLING NIGHT IN CANGONAMÁ WE woke up in the church narthex, thanked Padre Reyes and went up to move into our two room "apartment," which was over a little store. We met the owner and his family. Our suspicion was that maybe they had vacated the two rooms at the insistence of the Padre. But the owner assured us that was not the case. We negotiated the rent which came to sixty sucres a month or about $3.00 American, which at the time was worth about $27.00 in 21st century dollars. While this may seem a rip-off today, it was what he was happy to receive in return for the space. There was no running water, no outlets and just two electric light bulbs, one in each room, that generated about twenty-five to forty watts each on a good evening, if the town generator was working. The only running water was downstairs in the courtyard, and there was a shower spigot available with cold running water for our morning wakeups.

The place was filthy and we set about cleaning it up. We were still cleaning the next day when the owner from downstairs informed us that there was a stake truck going into Catacocha, a village down on the main highway about fifteen miles away from Playas, where the switchback road to our village met the highway. Since we needed food, cigarettes and supplies, we took advantage of whatever ride we could. Catacocha was small but big enough, at least, to have a store with things we would need to set up housekeeping such as food stuffs, pots, pans and some utensils.

The ride in the back end of the stake truck to Catacocha was uneventful, but the shopping trip opened our eyes to a few realities we hadn't anticipated. First of all, we were required to come up with the proper names for what we needed, so our Spanish was being challenged for the first time. Between the three of us, we managed to communicate well enough to get cans of tuna, some fruit and a few vegetables. We spent about $35, and I'm sure we made their day and maybe even their week with our purchases. All was going well until Joe asked if they had some *"bolsas de papel,"* paper bags, to carry our purchases. The look on the face of the clerk was something to behold. "Bags made of paper? Bags of paper?" I'm sure what he thought was, "Why would anyone put something heavy into a bag made from paper when every Ecuadorian had a nice *"alforja"* (woven cloth bag) to carry things in? These gringos must be crazy!" The use of a paper bag, something which we took for granted in everyday use (and long before plastic bags), had yet to arrive in Ecuador except for some of the very high-end supermarkets in Quito and Guayaquil. Even the concept of a "supermarket" was new to the country. But being the ever-polite Ecuadorian that he was, the clerk explained that all he had were sheets of newspaper to wrap our things in. How we carried them was up to us to figure out. We eventually managed to talk him out of some of the cardboard boxes that his supplies came in. This was for a price of course, as were the sheets of newspaper that were sold for home use - for certain hygienic needs.

Padre Reyes and Doug Strauss with me outside the church in Cangonamá.

Our two-room "apartment" on the upper level, in the center of the photo.

We hung around the little town until the truck was ready to return, but we learned we were to have companions. The truck was loaded with bags of rice and corn, the purchases of other passengers, and not a few chickens. And a wild assortment of passengers it was. We had a number of *campesinos* that worked for the hacienda in the valley below us, two families of indigenous natives, and a mother nursing her baby. All were comfortably sitting on the sacks of rice and corn, chatting amiably, and staring in wonder at the inconceivable sight of three gringos (three "*meesters*") riding along in the dusty twilight in the back of a truck. It was a dusty ride indeed, but I had a great sense of relief at the thought that there was at least one fairly easy way out of what seemed, up to now, a God forsaken place that had become our temporary home.

Joe chats with Fidelina and her daughter, Olga, in front of the parsonage.

SOCKING CLAVOS

THE MAIN PURPOSE OF OUR PRESENCE IN THIS FIRST ASSIGNED town was to see how we handled ourselves in the real world of community development. In essence, we were still being evaluated as we acclimated ourselves to living day to day in remote settings. In addition, we were to see what things our Yankee ingenuity could bring to improving the workflow and efficiency of the process and provide that "mid-level technical help" that the brochures talked about. The fact that we had three of us in this little town was a bit of overkill, but as it turned out Doug got an assignment to work on installing or improving a potable water system in the small village of Buena Vista, even further back in the mountains. Cangonamá was still to be his home base, but he would be heading out to that village for many of the days we were there. That left Joe and me to see what we could do.

The three of us had spent Sunday building shelves for our two rooms, getting an old table from the attic, putting away our supplies and generally making it livable, or as livable as it could be for three guys and the rooster who took up residence on the porch rail outside our door. He became our morning alarm clock. We had a small Coleman stove a little bigger than a large brief case; a five-gallon jug for water, boiled in advance and treated with our iodine pills; a few basic dishes and utensils; some pans to clean them in; and a few towels and washcloths. With our quarters settled, we were ready to get to work.

Our project, the partially constructed school as it appeared when we arrived.

Joe and I showed up at the worksite Monday morning. We introduced ourselves to the master carpenters (*maestros*) Panama and Bautista and to their two helpers. We asked what we could do to move things along. "Well, we are out of *clavos* (nails) so we can't get anything done until we get nails," they told us. "How long will that take?" we wanted to know. "*Quién sabe*?" (Who knows?) they said. "They were supposed to be delivered last week." We also noted a distinct lack of tools. Two saws, two hammers, a couple of chisels, a square and a plumb line with a chunk of chalk seemed to be the extent of the arsenal for the four of them. Building materials for the job were stacked about 300 feet away from the site. The superstructure to hold up what were to be poured cement columns looked like a jumble from the game, Pick-Up

Sticks, with all the poles and wood jutting out from them. We also noted stacks of used boards and poles all of which seemed to have a lot of nails sticking out. We decided we could pull out the nails, straighten them and have them available for immediate use.

To "pull out" is "*sacar*" (sock-car) in Spanish. Our first few days on the site consisted of Joe and me sitting on our backsides "*socking clavos*." We would pull them out and then hammer them back into shape to get them as straight as possible for re-use and then sent our recycled nails off to the workers. In cynical fashion, we started to wonder if this was really what we'd been prepared for all these months. Was this our "mid-level technical assistance?" At least this activity got them back in action, and Joe went up to the telegraph office (our thankfully discovered main link to the outside world) and sent off a telegram to the Loja office to let them know we needed nails and additional tools on the site. We needed them ASAP. We would soon learn how that translated in Ecuadorian culture.

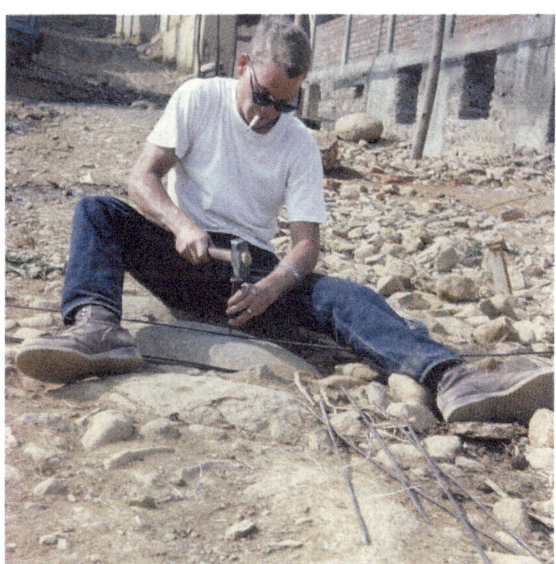

Joe Orr cuts rebar with a hammer and chisel.

We spent the rest of our days that week as basic laborers, moving the materials closer to the job site; forming stirrups for the rebar for the columns to be poured; cutting wire strands to tie them; and removing and cleaning the wooden forms that were used to hold the poured cement. One of the innovations or attractions of the schools we were helping to construct was that they were being built of brick and mortar and poured concrete columns and beams. Instead of adobe walls and dirt floors, they featured large, open windows with metal grillwork, cement floors, and built-in blackboards. In most cases, the new schools also contracted for new desks and chairs. Up to this point, classes in this village were held in individual homes with bad lighting, little furniture, and no facilities. When finished, the school would be the nicest, most modern building in the village. And it would be built with the help of the local community pitching in.

However, as we looked at the barefoot carpenter squaring off a wooden beam with an adze; watched the cement being mixed in a small trough and carried to the columns in five-gallon buckets one at a time; and the mud for the bricks being stirred in a donkey driven mixer, "modern" was the last word that came to mind. The mixer reminded me of Bible pictures of the thrashing floors. It consisted of a double thickness of three feet high, two and a half inch thick poles, driven into the ground in a circle with a five-foot thicker pole in the center of the circle. Attached to that vertical pole was a horizontal arm which had a halter that was put over the donkey's neck. Affixed to the bottom of the pole were the paddles that mixed the mud as the donkey walked around and around in circles. Although the two *maestros*, Panama and Bautista, were a delight to watch and listen to, they argued over every measurement and cut. While it was well intended and, we hoped, inspired by a desire to ensure quality construction, it severely slowed progress.

The archaic donkey driven mixer used to blend the clay and mud to make tiles and bricks.

A barefoot carpenter cuts a beam with an adze. And he still has ten toes!

In addition to our work on the project, we took some time out to show the school kids some organized games and let ourselves become known quantities to the community. To my surprise there were close to 230 kids "hidden away" in the various classrooms around the village. We also tried to encourage them to engage in some calisthenics, but the teachers, "*los profesores*," quietly let us know the kids were more interested in games than working out.

Three of the *profesores* showed up one evening and chatted for a while, and I found out that one of them had been exchanging correspondence with a pen pal from South Milwaukee. "Not so remote a village after all," I thought. It was an eye opener (and part of our education) that occasionally there are people who will surprise you with the extent of their knowledge, even in the outback. One of them entertained us with some guitar music and songs, and then they left for the evening, curiosity satisfied, I'm sure, as to how these three *Americanos* were getting along.

We thought maybe we could expedite the shipment of materials and get some tools (not to mention getting some "R&R") by personally heading into Loja. As no truck was scheduled to come through, we discovered another way to the highway in the valley, down the mountain on mule back. It sounded like a good idea at the time. We arranged for a boy to come at 5:45 a.m. with our trusty mounts, so we arose at 5:00, got ready and awaited his arrival. The appointed hour came and went as did 6:00, 6:15 and 6:30. Finally, showing little signs of remorse, he showed up about 6:45. The donkeys he brought had only pack saddles and, as we had no blankets, we used our jackets to cushion our backsides. It goes without saying, by the time we completed the two-hour journey down the mountain on our sure-footed but slow steeds, we were good and sore and looking forward to the cushioned ride on the bus. Unfortunately, due to our guide's late arrival, we missed that opportunity. We settled for the wooden benches of the next "*mixto*" that came along which was loaded with the normal mix of produce, passengers and animals. We managed to reach Catacocha by 11:00 and caught the 12:00 o'clock bus which traversed the 60-mile trip to Loja in a mere five and a half hours. This portion of the Pan-American "Highway" left a lot to the imagination, and its curves and turns and drop-offs exceeded anything that Disney had or has since come up with to provide sheer terror and breathtaking thrills and chills. When I finally reached my lodging, I took my first hot shower in two weeks, hit the sack and slept for 13 hours.

Doug and I on our way to Playas to catch the mixto.

Maestros Panama and Batista preparing for the installation of a beam.

REST, RECREATION AND REDEDICATION

WE THREE "CANGONAMÁNIANS" WERE SPREAD AROUND THE town, with Doug at a hotel, Joe staying with another Peace Corps Volunteer and I with a great guy, Jim Snyder, a seasoned professional civil engineer. Jim was seven years older than most of us and had both corporate and military experience. As a Volunteer he was assigned to the Loja Municipal Public Works. He had a pleasant, easy going, manner perhaps gained during his time working in Pearl Harbor with the U. S. Navy. Jim's knowledge and good sense of humor later proved to be a valuable resource and a calming presence in our midst.

On Sunday we went to Loja and shopped for food supplies and other necessities, attended a community picnic at a school, and I unintentionally slept through a dance that was held that night. I also picked up thirteen letters from Ann and a couple from home. Up to that point I had only received one letter and was feeling depressed with all that had occurred: the slow progress, poor diet, flea bites, pathetic transportation, and the general lack of communication. The letters from home perked me up.

Monday was Loja's Independence Day celebration and my notes regarding that day indicate that there was a big parade but, as usual, very disorganized. We, the assembled Peace Corps Volunteers, had our own party that night at the health Volunteers'

(Doris and Phyllis) house. While there we learned that John Mulligan, a New Yorker with an even heavier accent than Doug's, was in the hospital with amoebic dysentery. His plight was a reminder to us all, "don't drink the water!" The reality was that even in the "good" restaurants you might end up with lettuce or vegetables that had been washed in water that contained the amoebas, causing disease. And we did the best we could to be careful of what we ate.

Justo Andrade, the Ecuadorian Section Chief, had stopped by the night of the party and offered to take us back to Cangonamá on Tuesday but never showed up. Fortunately, John Smith came into town, and we made arrangements to go back with him and avoid another adventurous trip with the Provincial bus line. Smith gave us some extra money for the tools we needed, and with those obtained, we headed out at about noon on November 20th. John Smith was our first dinner guest. We feasted on a "real" meal of ham, potatoes, tomatoes and other goodies that we purchased in Loja...no goat meat, tough pork or bananas of any sort. Smith left the next day for Macará, a town in the southernmost part of Loja Province where Carmelo Cruz had ended up.

The next day the project engineer from the Ministry of Education showed up at the site and brought with him five carpenters who were to work on preparations for the roof. He read the riot act to our two *maestros* and said they had spent more on materials here than on any other job in the system. As a result, he put Joe and me in charge of allocating materials and accounting for the rest. I feared this would change the nature of the good relationship we had built up with the *maestros*, but it appeared it had to be done. The engineer, Ruilloba, was a true professional. (I never knew his first name.) A no nonsense guy, he was well-educated

Doug, John Smith and Joe experiencing one of our many commuting misadventures.

and truly dedicated to the projects under his purview. We were to gain great respect for him over the course of our stay in Ecuador. He was a barrel chested, five feet seven-inch tall man of about forty. He was one of those hard to pinpoint types. His uniform of the day was khaki pants, a long-sleeved collared shirt and a sturdy pair of boots which served him well in the varieties of terrains he covered. Engineer Ruilloba was the type of guy who would make a good running back. He sported that same level of energy and impatience to get things done.

On Friday, November 22nd, the carpenters who had come in with the engineer went to work on preparations for the roof. Two others were working with us building the forms for the *"vigas"* or beams. Work was progressing fairly smoothly, and our role as allocators didn't seem to be bothering anyone, so I was in a fairly bright mood. We had control, tools and supplies on hand, and a good number of workers to use them. Then at about 2:30

p.m. one of the workers asked, "How do you call the President of the United States?" I answered him, "Juan F. Kennedy. Why do you ask?" "He's died," he replied. I thought for a moment of the young, vigorous man who was President of the United States, smiled back and said, "You must be joking." Just then *Señor* Espinosa, the head of the local building committee, came by. Holding his hat in his hand, this tall, slim, elderly man said slowly and clearly with great sadness, "Someone has shot and killed your president. It was just on the radio."

I ran up to the room to see if I could get any news on my Zenith Trans-Oceanic radio, a valuable going away gift I received before leaving. My frustration and concern increased as I found the room was locked. I ran back down and got the key from Joe. "These guys say Lyndon Johnson is the President of the United States" I said, half in jest, still not wanting to believe it. I thought surely these people had misunderstood the news.

We both ran back up to the room and tuned in the Voice of America. "The President of the United States, John F. Kennedy, is dead," came the report. The details followed, and we could hardly believe what we heard about the events that had transpired in Dallas. It all seemed like a great fiction story, like something from Seven Days in May that I had just read and was partly inspired by events in Kennedy's Administration. We continued to listen to the reports until they became repetitive and decided to return to work and wait to see if further news would bring more clarity that night.

Although this event had global impact, here in the mountains of Ecuador life was going on as usual. This country had seen presidents come and go in numerous coups and assassinations. For example, between 1931 and 1940 there were twelve presidents. The most recently elected president had been overthrown by a military *junta* while our training was taking place. So perhaps to them it meant little. To us, and particularly to me, it meant a great deal.

My journal reflects my thoughts at the time. I noted how our great system of government can continue to function, and does function even in the face of such a tragedy. I thought about the new president and wondered how he would do. Most of all I thought and wrote about what President Kennedy had meant to me. I remembered about all he had done in the short time he had been in office and how he handled the Cuban Missile Crisis with great courage. Joe and I had big arguments about his efficacy as president and those discussions continue still today among political pundits. But none can deny the impact he had on the hearts and minds of the country. I remembered how I had actually been against Kennedy in the elections of 1960. Then, hearing his inaugural speech I had sat up and listened as millions of others had done and reflected to myself at that time, "This man may have something on the ball after all." Part of me said, "Let's see some action!" Kennedy was quick to point out that the action had to come from us, from the people. His "Ask not...." speech was, without a doubt as I've noted, why I found myself in Ecuador.

Perhaps full of patriotic fervor (or full of something else others might say) I noted this in my journal:

> His type of vision and his drive are what created, in a great degree, the Peace Corps. To my mind his death should be an incentive to the members of the Peace Corps to do a better job, to try harder in their work than they have ever done before. No matter what country one is from, or what his political views may be, one cannot fail to respect and admire this man for the progress he has made toward peace in this nuclear age and the "vigor," his famous word, with which he worked toward it. His death has caused for me a

> reflection on, and a rededication to, those principles of world peace, equality of man, and religious toleration to which he had dedicated his work. I hope now, that in my own way, and with God's help I can dedicate my life to making these principles a true reality.

I even acknowledged that this passage had been "possibly too verbose and too lofty," but I also noted that I hoped it would serve as a pinprick to my conscience to keep me on the road to these goals, "no matter what life may offer me in the years ahead." I must say I should have taken my journal out of storage more often over the years that have passed, for life offered me some amazing twists and turns that I hadn't anticipated. Over the years I fell far short of the lofty goals I set for myself that day. However, they kept me going for the short term in the months ahead that I had to spend in Ecuador.

A GENERAL FEELING OF MALAISE

ONE OF THE REASONS FOR THE INITIAL "IN COUNTRY" ASSIGNMENTS was to see how each Volunteer would adapt and cope with the culture, the work itself, the level of poverty and the general conditions under which they found themselves. For some who had slipped by the psychologists' scrutiny and judgments, this experience was the final deselection step. A few found it too much to take and returned to the States. Others got reassigned. The month of December was a time for group meetings and gatherings to provide feedback up the line on how the program was working and, no doubt, for the leaders and staff to take one more look at individuals and determine their next steps and placements. It was becoming clear to me that I didn't want to spend the rest of my two years on top of this mountain. My journal reflected a feeling of increasing gloom and frustration.

The days following Kennedy's assassination were slow. That weekend we walked around the town a little bit with the *maestros*, met a few more people in the town and played tourist taking some pictures for the folks back home. I planned to write a lot of letters in response to the ones I had received and initiate some others, including one to my former high school sweetheart, Sally Meyer, who had kindly remembered my birthday by sending me a card. But it was tough to get motivated as so much was involved with daily work, and since we could not mail things for a week or weeks at a time, it was easy to "put off until tomorrow." With Ann writing daily missives, guilt was setting in. Our food supplies were getting low; the weather was getting cold and foggy; and the fleas were continuing to attack me unmercifully.

On the job site, things were moving very slowly, but at least the school kids brought in a great number of wooden poles for supports and also a supply of rocks. This was part of the obligation for the community to supply materials and labor. The director of the school made a very patriotic speech; then the children placed the poles and rocks in piles, sang the national anthem and headed off to the classrooms in the various sites. We later found out that the wooden poles were donated by a man who lived back in the hills. The program paid fifteen cents per pole which went into a fund to buy things for the school. The director of the school received this money personally and spent it as he saw fit. I noted in my journal that this may account for his display of patriotism. My impression of him was that he looked like a "short, fat Mussolini type that would take you for all he could, given the chance."

The lack of organization on the job was getting to me as well. One day as I worked on the forms for the beams that would support the trusses, I was interrupted every five minutes by someone who asked me to hand something up to them. I was on my own as Joe and Doug had gone down the mountain to the highway on donkey back to meet two people. This was in response to a telegram we had received, informing us that "two gringo engineers were coming to Las Playas." We had no idea who they were or why they were coming. They turned out to be two Volunteers heading to another site and who, having no idea what it took to get to Cangonamá, just wanted to stop by and say hello!

On Thanksgiving, unbeknownst to us, a *minga* showed up to help pour the beams. The local *teniente politico* (local political

School children bringing in wooden poles for the school construction, as part of the town's required contribution.

A roofing specialist, above the clouds, prepares for the installation of the final beam on the school building. Note the use of keystone construction on the perpendicular beams.

official) herded them in, and I suspect it was probably under penalty of a fine if they didn't show up. Real community action! We scrambled to get to work, and we got the beam poured, working far into the night. Two days later, I noticed that we were low on bricks. The brick maker had not been paid for those he already delivered and was about to go on strike.

So, there I was: hungry, cold, flea bitten, and frustrated with the pace of work. I feared I was catching the "general malaise" that seems to affect most of the nonaffluent population of Ecuador. A lot has to do with Ecuador's history and the fact that even today sixty percent or more of its population lives below the poverty line. It is a country that has always been a "backwater country," an "also ran" in the broad history of South America. It probably had its heyday when Ecuador was still part of the Incan Empire that ran from Cuzco to Quito.

Feel free to skip the next chapter if you are not interested in my theory of the country's psyche.

A BRIEF HISTORY LESSON

TO UNDERSTAND ECUADORIAN PEOPLE AND THEREFORE THE Ecuadorian mentality, it might be helpful to know a little about the history and geography of the country. While Ecuadorians are intensely proud of their country, they are also aware that it hasn't had a lot of "wins." In fact, the last time they won a war was probably the time when Atahualpa, ruler of the northern portion of the Incan empire, defeated Huascar, the ruler of the southern portion of the empire, headquartered in Cuzco, Peru, in the Battle of Riobamba in 1532. This was still a source of national pride to Ecuadorians as one of the rare instances when "Ecuador" forcefully bettered a neighboring country. Shortly after that battle, the newly arrived Spaniards captured Atahualpa and held him for ransom. In 1533, the Incas filled a room with gold and silver as ransom anticipating his release but Hernando Pizarro, seeing the room was filled, promptly killed Atahualpa. He then proceeded to capture the southern kingdom in Cuzco and later, joined by other forces, the northern capital of Quito.

For about the next two hundred years Ecuador was a small part of Spain's colonies called New Granada. New Granada included what is now Columbia, Venezuela, Panama, Northern Peru, part of Northwestern Brazil, and sections of Surinam and the Guyanas. At that time portions of Ecuador's territory extended into the Amazon. I was often reminded, and the Ecuadorian literature and history books were filled with the fact, (and what all students were taught) that Ecuador *"es, ha sido, y siempre será un pais Amazónico,"* (Ecuador "is, has been, and always will be an Amazonian country.") While they did little to develop it, Ecuador lost a large part of their Amazonian territory to the Peruvians in the 1943 war. By 1963, the hurt and humiliation and resentment over that loss still persisted. This area, the *Oriente,* was and is known mostly for its fierce native tribesmen including the Aucas and the Jivaros. It appears that every time Ecuador sought to add to their territory by means of force, whether it was with Colombia or Peru, they lost.

During the colonial period the most common form of land ownership was a feudal system called the *encomienda.* Under this system a colonist or soldier was given a portion of land and the indigenous people who lived on it to work it. They didn't call it slavery, but a rose by any other name is still a rose. The landowners were feudal lords; the Indians were their slaves and treated as such. By the early 17th century there were about 500 such *encomiendas.* The system enslaved about half of the native Ecuadorians which equaled about half the population of the entire country. Some of the *haciendas* were very large, but most were smaller than those found in other parts of South America at the time. There were a number of attempts to reform the system but it endured until the end of the colonial era.

As Spain went, so went its colonies. In the 1700's Spain suffered a major depression and so did Ecuador. Textiles, a major export, dropped anywhere from fifty to seventy-five percent between 1700 and 1800. Ecuador's cities fell into ruin. The elite landowners were reduced to selling off their lands, their jewelry, and other possessions. The indigenous population who had been enslaved improved their lot somewhat by transitioning to work on the remaining haciendas or by returning to their communal villages in the mountains and valleys of the land. The deterioration of both the economy and infrastructure of the country was compounded by the expulsion of the Jesuits in 1767, ordered by King Charles III of Spain. The Jesuits had established over thirty-six missions in the territory. And they, along with a number of successful schools and hospitals, all went into ruin as well.

By the early 1800's what is now Ecuador was a land of poor ex-landowners, poor *mestizos* (a mix of Spanish and indigenous people), a poor enslaved or subservient indigenous population, and a small handful of elites into whose hands power and control resided. By 1963 not much had changed, except for the exceptional method of governing this "happy land."

I'll spare you the details of the fight for independence in Latin America in the 1800's. However, Ecuador's fight provides some history that is instructive in understanding the nature of the country. It involves that "wonderful" vehicle of Latin American politics known as the *"coup"* or *"coup d'etat"* closely followed by the ruling *"junta"* of military rulers. Much of the history has to do with the Creoles or, in Spanish, the *"Criollo."* The people from Spain were known as *"Peninsulares,"* high class individuals born in Spain but became permanent residents. *Criollos* in the "caste system" of Latin America were full-blooded Spaniards born in Spanish colonies. They were a step below the *Peninsulares,* but of higher status or rank than *mestizos,* those of mixed Spanish and indigenous bloodlines. *Criollos* could have up to one-eighth indigenous blood in their ancestry and not lose their social place. A large part of Latin America's fight for independence had its roots in resentment on the part of the *Criollos* of the special privileges given to Spanish born individuals.

In 1808 (when Napoleon put his brother on the Spanish throne) Quito's *Criollos,* who supported Spain's King Ferdinand, overthrew the ruling *Peninsulares,* fearing that they might recognize Napoleon's brother's legitimacy to the throne. History says it quickly became apparent that the *Criollos* overestimated their local support, and when the *Peninsulares* arrived, they quickly and peacefully capitulated and turned the rule back over to the loyalists. In spite of assurances to the contrary, the Spanish authorities, in their search for participants, meted out harsh punishment to guilty and innocent alike.

This punishment led to another *Criollo* led riot in 1810, the result of which was the formation of a majority, *Criollo* heavy, ruling *junta*. In 1811, the *junta* called for a congress and approved a constitution. It declared the entire province of Ecuador, called at the time, the *Audiencia de Quito,* to be independent of the current (then French) government in Spain. The constitution also provided for democratic governing institutions for the *Audiencia*. The *junta* then decided to launch a military invasion against the loyalists to the south in Peru. However, their forces, while enthusiastic, were poorly trained and ill equipped against the Viceroy's army, and the Quito rebellion was crushed in 1812.

In the 1820's Ecuador was in turmoil. It was the battle ground for forces loyal to Spain and forces that wanted to be part of the newly formed Gran Columbia, a state established in about 1819. It encompassed Panama, Colombia, Ecuador, and parts of Venezuela. Some favored independence for the *Audiencia*; some wanted to join forces with Peru; and others favored the status quo. Ecuador was swept up in the fight for independence from Spain and in 1830 became an independent nation with Juan Jose Flores, a Venezuelan born, military man as its first president.

Flores had been appointed Governor of Ecuador by Simon Bolivar during Ecuador's association with Gran Columbia. He appeared more interested in military adventures against Columbia, drained the treasury, and by 1845 was ousted by an insurrection in Guayaquil that drove him from power and the country.

One historian stated "that the next 15 years were the most turbulent in the country's...history." I would say take your pick. By the time I arrived in Ecuador, the presidency had changed hands fifty-seven times in its 133-year history as an independent country. Eleven of those changes were in the fifteen years from 1845 to 1860 and another eleven, as previously mentioned, between 1931 and 1940. Sometimes the terms in office were as short as two or three months, before some party, some group, or someone with a gun chose to make a term ending "Change in Administration." Many of these changes were (and are) driven by geography and many by commercial interests. It was the liberals of the coast in Guayaquil versus the conservatives of the Andes in Quito or the military versus the leftists. Name the cause and you will probably find one representative who held office supporting it.

Geography has a lot to do with the mentality of the country as well. There is a legend that when God was making the Western Hemisphere, He started out in Alaska and worked south. When He came to South America, He went down the east coast with His building materials all the way to the southern tip of South America. Then He worked his way north again, but when He got almost to Panama, He discovered that He had too much material, and in a fit of pique He threw it all down in a great pile, and that's how He made Ecuador. And it is quite a mix. The hot steamy lowland coastal area borders the Pacific with Guayaquil and Esmeraldas as its base and central focus. The rugged Andes Mountains, with snowcapped volcanoes and lush, green valleys in between the majestic peaks, run from north to south through the country. To the east of the Andes lie the river filled jungle areas that border the Amazon region. The coastal people are a mix of commercial-minded, enterprising businessmen involved in commerce, fishing and the growing of produce; and poor indigenous and mixed-race descendants of slaves from the early colonial period. The Andes are home to Quito, the capital, in the north; centrally located Cuenca in the middle; and Loja in the south. Other cities, towns and pueblos of lesser size are scattered along the winding and torturous Pan-American Highway that runs between them but doesn't necessarily connect them. Here live the conservative folk carrying on the culture and customs left by their Spanish forefathers as well as the majority of the indigenous Amerindian population living in poverty in the hills, nooks and crannies of the mountains. To the east is the *Oriente*, the "almost" Amazon area - full of rivers, full of unmet promise, and the primary domain of native Indian cultures.

The long-established "caste system" that I mentioned before is based not only on ethnicity but also on the area of the country in which people live. My reflection in 1963 was that the coastal people thought the Andean people too conservative and too slow to change. The conservatives of the Andes thought the coastal people either as too liberal or too lazy and too much of a mixed-race bunch to amount to anything. Together they all looked down on the native indigenous descendants of the Incas and the tribal people of the *Oriente*. The country in 1963 was about 4.5 million people, about six per cent of whom were white, 65 per cent mestizo or mixed race, 25 per cent indigenous, and four per cent a mixture of black and mixed race Indian/black backgrounds. At the top of the system are the whites of Spanish descent, who control or try to control the politics and major businesses of the country; then the mestizo population, many of whom have risen from the laboring class to form the bulk of small business owners and merchants; and at the bottom, the bulk of the population who are those involved primarily in labor, subsistence farming and other agricultural activities. Trying to get the men who have risen from the laboring class to the merchant or entrepreneurial class involved in our voluntary labor projects or *mingas* was a major challenge for the Volunteers, as doing manual labor was seen as a step backward rather than as an act of civic pride or contribution.

The country is 95 per cent Catholic, and 65 per cent percent or more of the population lives in poverty. They are used to doing so. Any politician (or Peace Corps Volunteer) promising that things will be different or that there is hope, has a tough sell. "Fool me once," they say, "shame on you. Fool me twice, shame on me!" They have seen presidents and *juntas* come and go at the highest levels and nothing changes. They've seen and heard politicians at the local level make promises and nothing changes. Even the well-intentioned politicians run into an entrenched bureaucracy that seems intent on pouring sand into the wheels of progress. A word I was to hear often was *"fregado"* – the situation was very *fregado*; everything is a mess, a muddle, very annoying. Or in more vulgar terms everything is *jodido!* Everything is screwed up (or worse), and the implication is it can't be fixed. I was soon to learn how *fregado* things could get and just where this "malaise" (that started this history lesson) originated.

ROUND 'EM UP AND MOVE 'EM OUT!

As November ended and the cold winds of December started to blow, the time in our initial assignment was thankfully coming to an end. The work was slowing down, due to the lack of the brickmaker being paid on time. Each day a cold, thick fog rolled in, enveloping everything in sight. Visibility was reduced to about 100 feet. The cold winds necessitated wearing our coats in the apartment on a regular basis, the fleas were still biting and our food supplies were running low. Doug, Joe and I had been subsisting on tuna and noodles for a while. We decided to walk around to see what we could find and, after hitting every "store" (picture one room store fronts) in this little pueblo, we ended up with a half dozen rolls and two eggs. We mixed up a sauce of tomato paste, tuna, mayonnaise and parmesan cheese, poured it over spaghetti, and that was what we had for our Thanksgiving dinner.

We were still performing menial tasks and not learning much new about the process, so we were glad to receive a telegram announcing that a meeting would soon be held in Loja to let us provide feedback on what we had learned and receive information about our new and more permanent assignments. We were happy to hear that but had hoped it might be in Cuenca, a larger city with more amenities and opportunities to do some much-needed Christmas shopping. Later in the day we received a second telegram saying the meeting would indeed be in Cuenca on Monday and that we should therefore leave on Saturday. I was so happy to hear that news it was almost as if we were going home.

We again needed to take the mule route down to Playas. We made sure to leave the key to the apartment for Doug with the Padre's housekeeper, Fidelina, as Doug was still working on a road project in Buena Vista back in the hills. Keys were often an issue. One padlock, one key and no convenient corner hardware store to make duplicates. Keys, or lack thereof, would come to play a large part in some of my adventures.

Before we left, the priest and Fidelina reminded (or rather, told) us that we should remember to bring back gifts for them. We rode on the top of one of the *mixtos* to Catacocha which proved to be the better part of the trip to Loja. The bus we boarded there was filled with students from a Catholic girls' school in Macará who sang school songs at the top of their lungs for the three-plus hour trip into town. That, along with the cramped seating, guaranteed that I arrived in Loja with a massive headache.

Bill Shorn (in sunglasses on left), Chuck Jennings (in cowboy hat), Frank Gates, Nobel Wiltshire, Joe Orr and Tom Roan ignoring one of the many indigenous beggars at a square in Cuenca.

Joe and I left Loja the next day at 9:00 along with five other area Volunteers and arrived in Cuenca around 4:30 in the afternoon. We met with some of the others for dinner who had gathered for the meeting and learned, with increasing levels of envy, about their accommodations and assignments. They were living in big houses with hot baths. They had contacts with the engineers on a regular basis, and were doing almost no physical labor. Tough news for us after having been "*socking clavos*" for hours a day, taking cold showers and eating canned tuna and noodles.

The next day we received the news that our big chiefs could not fly in from Quito due to the cloud cover. That gave us a vacation day! I took advantage of the free time and asked Doc Caplin if he could give me anything for my flea bites, as I felt like a walking scab. All that he could recommend was taking a hot shower at his place. I took him up on his offer, and one really hot shower helped shrink my myriad of scabs from the bites.

We went out as a group to a restaurant for lunch, and I was again made aware of the variety of places and restaurants that the Volunteers in the Cuenca area could access. The Alaska, our one little "safe house" restaurant in Loja, would never be the same. The Alaska was run by a German ex-pat who kept a very clean operation and offered a "Peace Corps approved" menu that even included ice cream. However, it did not match the quality nor variety available in Cuenca which was, by comparison, a very cosmopolitan city.

We checked back in at the office and discovered that the chiefs had still not arrived, so we went out to the rental home of Volunteers Chuck Jennings and Tom Roan in Baños, a town that featured the natural hot baths from whence it got its name. There were three spring fed pools with water temperature between 75 to 85 degrees and about 120 degrees at the entrance. We took full advantage of those amenities in the afternoon. After a month and a half of cold showers, it was heaven – two hot water experiences in one day!

After our visit to Baños, I had the best dinner in Cuenca that I had eaten in Ecuador. The dinner included chateaubriand with mushrooms and all the trimmings, all for about $1.75. It was a treat and a far cry from our fare for the last month in Cangonamá. We wrapped up the evening wandering through the streets with Chuck strumming on his guitar, our group serenading the populace with folk songs; making a quick stop at a liquor store; and partying far into the night at the Doc's pad. It was all a welcome escape from the last couple of months, even if it had to be paid for with a hangover the following morning when the chiefs finally arrived for the meeting.

It was a very good meeting. We provided our complaints and feedback, asked and answered questions, received some very useful advice and books explaining all phases of construction, however belated. In the process my admiration and respect for James Watson, the Program Director, was greatly increased at the time. He impressed me as a very dedicated, energetic, even if sometimes crude, individual.

We received our new assignments. Joe was assigned to Cera, a small town very close to Loja. I received the news that my new assignment would be "La Toma," or Catamayo as it is officially called, a town just south and west on the other side of the mountain that bordered Loja. I had been through it on my travels to and from Cangonamá. It was much closer to Loja, and I was thrilled. We wrapped up the session by doing a little Christmas shopping at the local shops and then bowling at a "serviceable" bowling alley with crude lanes, but it was a great diversion.

I returned to Loja the next day and put up at a hotel. Joe arrived the next morning with John Smith and informed me that he was going to stay and wait for his orientation trip around construction sites with the Engineer Ruilloba and that Smith would give me a ride out to Cangonamá. I had plans for a bit more shopping and maybe a long overdue haircut, but a ride with the boss sure beat another adventure on a crowded bus and a slow donkey ride up the mountain. This was the start of what turned out to be the "long goodbye to Cangonamá."

When Smith and I got to Catacocha, about two-thirds of the way back, it dawned on me that Doug might still be at his project in Buena Vista and that Joe had forgotten to give me the key to the apartment. When we arrived in Cangonamá I checked with the priest's assistant and learned that Doug, indeed, had the key and was long gone. I informed *Señor* Espinosa, the man who had told us about Kennedy's assassination and who lived across the street from our place, about my plight. He graciously offered to let me stay at his home that evening, and I gladly accepted. He gave me a room and a bed and offered a meal which he was reluctant to serve as he knew we "eat different" than they do. I wanted to say, "No, we eat the same things you do, but it's clean and free of bacteria." But that was obviously not what I said. No doubt the word may have gone out, as well, that our garbage was full of tuna cans. I sent a telegram to Doug telling him to send the key with someone the next day.

I received a return telegram in the morning informing me that no one was headed out our way that day. I thought to myself, "Well, here we go on the amoeba diet." So far, the meals Sr. Espinosa had provided had all been pretty good. I was just hoping that he had been bringing to a boil the soup and coffee he had been serving. I had been giving English lessons to his teen age daughter over the weeks there and spent the afternoon doing that, as well as reading one of the books that I had brought along.

Jim Snyder and Doug returned the next day at 5:00, but not

before I was served some coffee with milk. I found out the milk had come directly from Sr. Espinosa's cow - directly from his cow. I remembered the Doc's prediction that drinking unpasteurized milk was a sure route to intestinal cancer. However, "When in Rome, do as the Romans do." Joe came in around 8:00 falling all over himself for forgetting to give me the key. We set about deciding how to split up our possessions among the three of us so we could pack in as much as possible with Engineer Ruilloba's Jeep the next day.

When he arrived, we stuffed what we could of our belongings into the Jeep and then had to figure out what to do with the rest of our things - what was to stay and how we could get the rest down the mountainside. It was getting hectic. We were also packing suitcases for our respective Christmas breaks as well as deciding what would go into storage in Loja in preparation for our moves to the next locations. And there was still work to be done. The weather was getting even colder and wetter, and the workers were angry about having been chastised by Ruilloba and the Padre for lack of progress and the general slowness of their work. (Something we had said in our reports in Cuenca perhaps coming back to haunt us?) Nobody, it seemed, was happy about nuttin'!

The next afternoon at around 5:00 I saw *Maestro* Panama coming down the hill looking very dejected. The priest and local honchos wanted him and the crew to finish pouring a beam. The *minga* (I think a forced one) had left at 4:00 and so had the school kids who had been "helping." They had been passing up coffee can size loads of cement up the ladders. So, Joe and I pitched in, and then finally, a few of the townspeople (true volunteers) showed up and we used big five-gallon buckets to pass the cement up the ladders. We all worked hard and perspiration was pouring as if we had been in a ten-round fight. Night fell, the lanterns appeared, and it turned into a rather fun community event which we finished in good time. As was the custom, it was celebrated with passing around shots of "*trago.*" *Trago* just means drink, but in this part of Ecuador it customarily means a shot glass of the hot, burning cane liquor (think of a cross between moonshine and Greek ouzo without the anise) that seemed to be the staple of any social activity in Ecuador.

The following day we continued packing up and said our goodbyes over a few beers with the *maestros,* who finally and reluctantly returned the Peace Corps hammers and saws we had lent them. That evening Doug, Jim Snyder (who had been helping Doug), Joe and I had a very nice dinner with the Padre, Fidelina, and her daughter, Olga. We also gave them the presents that they had requested. They were well pleased with the simple but meaningful items we picked out, and we were rewarded by their sincere appreciation. We returned to our quarters and hit the sack (flea filled) for the last time in this dreary little spot in the mountains.

At 3:30 in the morning we were awakened to the horrendously loud squealing of a pig that was being slaughtered on a doorstep just up the road from our place. Who knows? Maybe it tastes better if prepared by the light of the moon. We got back to sleep and at 6:15 and were awakened again by the roar of the truck that was to take us and our belongings to Playas. The man with whom we had arranged to use the truck had told us he would send someone over to tell us when it was almost ready to go. He hadn't. We jumped out of our beds and had to scramble to split up our belongings. We threw the dirty laundry into suitcases, dismantled and folded the cots, and threw the whole mess into the truck by 7:00. We got down to Playas in time to catch the bus, but only after three pigs were loaded on the truck at a stop on the way down. We unloaded our belongings and waited, along with too many others, for the *mixto* that was to arrive at 8:30. At about 8:45 it came along, loaded with pigs, firewood, people and cargo. There was absolutely no place for our belongings so we opted to wait for the school bus type *Cooperativa* transport from Macará, hoping (in my case) that it would be devoid of singing school girls.

The bus finally arrived about 10:30 and it too was packed, but we found room for our things on top and squeezed into the crowded bus. At last, we were on our way. Adios to Cangonamá! We went about one mile and the bus dropped its transmission.

Men loading live pigs onto a mixto.

Two hours later another *mixto* came by loaded with oil drums, but we found enough room for our belongings among them and finally got into Catacocha at about 1:00 in the afternoon. We waited until about 2:30 when another Cooperative bus came along that was full inside and loaded on top. We managed to get our stuff on top; and I squeezed myself inside and sat on a wooden box placed between two seats. I rode that way for two hours until the bus was stopped. Then we waited for two Caterpillar bulldozers to cut out a path on the side of the mountain so the bus could proceed. This was the construction going on as part of the building of the Pan-American Highway. We waited in the rain inside that hot, smelly bus for about an hour and finally reached La Toma (also known as Catamayo) by 6:30, about three hours behind schedule. There, we were informed that a bus had gone off the road somewhere south of town and that we would have to wait until an ambulance went by so it would have room on the highway.

We decided to go into a restaurant to order some dinner. Just as our food was being served, about twenty minutes later, the ambulance came through and we were told we had to leave immediately. We left our dinners sitting on the table and were on our way.

Within fifteen minutes we hit the fog in the mountain between La Toma and Loja. We proceeded the rest of the way on this under-construction, winding, mountain road at about ten to fifteen miles per hour. After thirteen and a half hours of travel, we finally reached Loja at 8:30. The town had never looked so good. Cangonam*á* was behind me. La Toma lay ahead, and in between was a very much anticipated Christmas break in Quito.

CHRISTMAS IN QUITO & BEYOND

AFTER A COUPLE DAYS OF RECOVERY AND PREPARATION IN LOJA, I rode on another very packed bus for an eight-hour trip north to Cuenca. There I met some other Volunteers who shared their plans for their vacations, some of which included trips to Columbia to reconnect with some of the female Volunteers from training days - better plans than mine, for sure. A few of us caught the movie *Psycho* (which I had seen with a summer love when it first came out in 1960) at the one and only local theater. In spite of the fact that the theater was old, not well maintained, and had hard wooden seats, it was still a wonderful form of escapism.

The next day, December 22nd, we got up at about 3:30 a.m. in order to catch the 4:30 bus to Quito. Gerry Mussett and I sat together in a three-person bench seat. Gerry, whose assignment was in Loja, was an irascible sort of guy. He could be a lot of fun but easily angered. It was our bad luck to be on one of the old, wood framed, dusty, rickety conversion busses. At first it was not crowded at all, but as we gathered additional passengers on this ticketed ride, things began to change. A <u>very</u> large woman holding a drooling, one-year old toddler discovered she was in the wrong seat and, wouldn't you know, her seat was next to ours by the window. She was dressed in the manner which most indigenous women of the Ecuadorian Andes sported whether winter or summer. She wore a dusty black Fedora, what appeared to be layers and layers of woolen skirts and a heavy black poncho. She waddled over and pushed and squeezed her very large body into the space and propped her toddler on her lap, leaving the equivalent of one space for Gerry and me. I moved over to another seat, but the bus took on more and more passengers including another lady and her baby who took the seat on the other side of Gerry. He was getting angrier and angrier. I could tell by the look on his face that Gerry was about to become a very ugly American. I took pity on him and offered to switch seats and take his place before he did something drastic. Gerry declined, since he had already complained in no uncertain terms to the driver when we had stopped for a food break. The driver said we could sit in the seats up by him after we reached the next stop in Riobamba. We gladly took him up on his offer.

As I moved my things forward and went to arrange my coat as a pillow, I noticed my wallet was gone. I notified the driver and he told me to go back and look around the seat and floor where I had been sitting and I did so. But the "fat lady from the circus" refused to move so I could take a thorough look. I couldn't find anything around the area and notified the driver that was the case. He proceeded to announce for all to hear that I had lost my wallet on the bus. With that announcement it could have been picked up by anyone, but my bet was still on the big lady. Even when we stopped and I went to look on the bus again, she refused to move. I was pissed. I was angry with myself, angry with the collective Ecuadorian populace and feeling very sorry for myself. "You come down to help these people out and you get robbed, overcharged and heckled from one end of the country to the other," say my notes of the time. In retrospect, no real damage was done except the bother of replacing a number of documents and a little money, as I did have the good sense to use a money belt for the trip. But this was supposed to be "the season to be jolly" and I sure wasn't. We were coming up on just two months in the country and my attitude was not good. I was flea bitten and, unlike many of my more fortunate fellow Volunteers, had been stuck in some nowhere town in what seemed to be a very disorganized operation. I was feeling pretty misunderstood and unappreciated by the populace for our efforts. And now I had been robbed. I was angry and wallowing in a good bit of self-pity. This was certainly not in the spirit of Christmas.

We got into Quito about 7:00 that evening and went to check into our hotel where we were to meet Joe Orr, Chuck Jennings, and Tom Roan. They had come up on another carrier, the "high-end" Pullman Carchi (newer school busses with more comfortable seats). They left an hour after we had but arrived forty-five minutes earlier than we did, primarily because, in my thinking, their driver did not stop for every Tom, Dick and Pedro along the way. They weren't at the hotel to meet us. After a while we figured out that they weren't there because the hotel was full. We went to the other Peace Corps approved hotel, found them there, and Gerry and I registered for the duration of our time in Quito. Other Volunteers whom we hadn't seen since the initial training and orientation began to roll in. My spirits rose at least a little bit as it began to seem like old home week. We swapped stories, gathered for breakfast, lunch and dinner, and even shopped at a real, true-to-life American type supermarket. According to my notes it even smelled like one. We stopped by the Peace Corps offices and half kiddingly told the Office Secretary, Diane Hawkins, that we were going to have a party at her house on Christmas Eve. We topped off the 23rd by going to see *White Christmas* at the local movie theater. This, at least, provided me a sense of familiar Christmas tradition.

I had been anticipating this break more than I knew. As you may have noted, more than a little self-pity and cynicism had been creeping into my psyche and my comments. There was within me a loneliness in the midst of all this much anticipated break in spite of the fact that I was with and among companions. Maybe it was the fact that Ann had been around during our training and much of my free time, when it was available, was spent with her. Maybe I would have bonded more closely with some of the other guys had that not been the case.

Some were interested in bonding, others not so much. Looking back on it, we Volunteers were an interesting mix of independent, mostly self-confident and, in some cases, visionary people. Those who were possessed with solid engineering skills moved ahead in a more clinical, detached manner, more demonstrating by example rather than teaching a skill. While those with softer skills and a vision of what could be (such as myself) hoped to achieve results by building relationships, cajoling, teaching, influencing others toward achieving their own self-sufficiency.

In some instances, these initial assignments led some of my companions to openly talk about quitting and going home. Around the drinking tables at this Christmas time more than a few expressed that intention, having experienced similar levels of frustrations as had I. Part of that may have been driven by home sickness. For others it was, I think, a sense that the Peace Corps experience was "not as advertised." I think they had expected to be welcomed with open arms and were frustrated with the lack of organization and progress. In spite of attempts to achieve a holiday atmosphere there was some hollowness in the partying, as this was for most of us, our first Christmas away from home. It was just not the same. We missed our loved ones. But we partied on, out of habit or necessity, to try and make it feel like it was "home."

Much of the time in Quito was spent eating and drinking and making connections for the next phase of our work and travels. This was, in a way, our "interregnum" that period between two regimes or two kings, a time of anticipation, not sure of what was coming next. We had had our initial assignments, had been given our next, but hadn't gotten there yet. Back home the government was going through its own "change of regime" following Kennedy's assassination, but all of that seemed far away and, in truth, it was. We'd experienced very little of the shock, trauma and mourning that occurred back home. I made arrangements for a call to Ann on the 24th but it went badly. The reception was poor, I probably didn't say the right things, and it cost twenty-two dollars to make the call. In spite of it all, it was nice to have a touch of home.

Christmas Eve was spent at Diane's home as we had "threatened." Our hostess was very willing to be so. She was a lovely lady about thirty, divorced, with a ten-year-old daughter and a boy about seven, popular with the guys in a friendly way, an angel of mercy to many. But the party consisted of too many guys drinking too much and not enough girls. It was pretty much a bust until we went off to Midnight Mass and then came back. We danced and partied until 3:00. I slept in Christmas morning.

According to my journal notes, Christmas day was a bore. I had a hamburger around noon, wrote some letters, and read a little. I later joined some of the other guys, and we went to the Hotel Quito for dinner, hung out at Diane's for a bit and then went up to the Quito Casino for a nightcap in a final effort to celebrate. It didn't work. My spirits were like the rainy, grey weather that contributed to my depressed attitude. I wasn't looking forward to another Christmas alone nor going back to Loja.

The next day was a day of renewal. I spent the morning at the Peace Corps office, a practice which was becoming our routine. Gerry and Dave Hess joined me, and we later played tourist by walking around taking pictures and picking up travel brochures. In my case, it was in anticipation of a trip around South America that Ann and I had been planning. I later went to the Brazilian Embassy to take care of some paperwork and reserve a flight in anticipation of Ann's arrival. I arrived at 4:00 and waited until 5:00 for an agent to show up but to no avail so I decided it was time to reward myself with a real Christmas dinner.

Gerry and I went to the Hotel Colón, a place about one block from the U. S. Embassy, often frequented by Americans. This night was no exception. The atmosphere and the music were beautiful, and I had the new best meal I had eaten since arriving in Ecuador: soup, followed by a raspberry juice appetizer, filet mignon with all the trimmings, rosé wine and, to top it all off, two chocolate sundaes. On this quiet Quito evening, we walked back to our hotel through a light drizzle. For the first time while on this vacation I felt good and at peace. I decided the Hotel Colón was the charm. "Perhaps a good place to go and/or stay when Ann arrives," I thought to myself.

Ever the skinflint when it comes to money, I decided to stay over to avoid having to spend $14.00 for the flight to Guayaquil on a commercial airline the next day. It was only $7.00 on TAME (Transportes Aéreos Militares Ecuatorianos), the quasi-military airline that was formed by the Ecuadorian Air Force in 1962 using old DC-3's for civilian use. Their schedule was irregular and they didn't fly every day. On a salary of $100.00 per month, you save where you can.

I was finally able take care of business at the Brazilian embassy, signing the necessary documents to get the visas for our trip and making the flight reservations for Ann. Then I mailed off the Christmas presents I had bought, and purchased a little $8.00 point-and-shoot camera. It would allow me to send pictures home more often than my 35-millimeter rolls of film could provide and prevent my having to deal with the light meter and camera settings for every shot.

The next day, December 28th, I flew down to Guayaquil at 7:30 in the morning and headed for the Peace Corps offices. I wanted to check in and get my bearings as this was my first exposure to Guayaquil, a city with a totally different atmosphere, climate and culture from the Andean mountains where I had spent my time so far. It was definitely tropical - hot and humid. It was dirty, with visible signs of poverty all around. As you fly in you can literally smell the muggy difference in the air. But we were not there to work, thank goodness. This was still Christmas vacation and we made the most of it. I met up with Dave Hess, Ed Delci, Tom Roan and a few other Volunteers, and we checked in at the Hotel Espanõla. It looked a lot like the Air Force barracks in Albuquerque where we had our preventative dental work done during training. The rest of the guys took off for parts unknown and some well-known.

In Ecuador, government regulated prostitution was available to anyone "of age" and willing to pay the price. Some of the Volunteers certainly fit that profile, either out of curiosity or due to biological drive. The government figured these brothels were preferable to back alley "whore houses" which were a public health menace. They were run sort of like a casino without gambling tables. The curious could go there, buy over-priced drinks and listen to the music, but that clearly was not the norm.

Ed Delci and I decided to play tourist again. Ed was a wiry guy, smart and full of energy. From Chandler, Arizona, he was the only Latino in our group. His outgoing character, inherent facility with the language, and penchant for overcoming any obstacles in his way endeared him to the people of Solano, the town to which he was initially assigned. Ed and I walked along the waterfront taking pictures of the SS HOPE hospital ship which was in the harbor, took in two soccer games (the second of which got rained out), and we ate a lot. Guayaquil had a number of sidewalk cafes that featured *ceviche* (shrimp cocktail), roasted corn kernels, and very good Pilsner beer in very large bottles. We took advantage of those as well as a great soda fountain, much like those found at home, called the "Milko Bar." It was run by a U. S. ex-pat female who looked like one of my former U. W. girlfriends and who seemed really tired. Having worked on the late-night shift at The Corner, a frozen custard stand near my hometown, I could identify. We played some "North American" songs on the juke box and cheered her and ourselves up by ordering two hamburgers and a banana split each. Then it was back to the hotel and preparation for a new adventure - a return by Jeep through the coastal jungles and up through the foothills of the Andes to Cuenca.

Ed, Tom and I left at about noon in the Jeep that belonged to the local Peace Corps secretary, Pat Conger. We saw a lot of beautiful scenery, the banana groves along the way and an amazing variety of plants. Unfortunately, since Pat chose to stop at so many spots along the way to collect samples of those plants, we did not arrive in Cuenca until 10:00 that evening. However, the trip had been made even more memorable as we were able to see a beautiful sunset and a full moon shining on the clouds as we climbed through the Andes. I bunked at Ed's for the night.

On New Year's Eve, 1963, I went over to the Cuenca Peace Corps office and picked up my travel pay and saw that my Peace Corps footlocker had arrived. This was a Christmas present! I received a two burner Coleman cookstove, a cot, a canteen, a dishpan, a cook kit and a lantern. (I now had two lanterns since Joe and I had divided up belongings as we left Cangonam*á*.) To top it all off, they also included a four-foot wooden level with brass trim. I arranged to have the locker sent down to Loja. We went to a party at Ed's landlord's that night and the White Horse

Whiskey started flowing freely. We witnessed the local custom of welcoming in the New Year watching "*Ano Viejo*," a dummy figure representing the Old Year that is burned in the middle of the street at midnight. I was thinking it was pretty neat, but a long way from what I would rather be doing at midnight on New Year's Eve. We stayed around drinking and dancing and finally hit the hay at 2:00.

I stuck around Ed's on New Year's Day after recovering, or attempting to recover, from a very bad hangover. By 12:30, I was pretty much alive again when Ed came in and reminded me that we were supposed to go to his landlord's again for lunch at 1:00. We had quite the feast and I became an "*inocente*" when I discovered a plastic fig in my food. This is much like the custom during Mardi Gras where one finds the plastic baby within the King Cake. If you are the *inocente* you are the butt of a lot of jokes and the family seemed delighted that the *gringo* had been "had." They play little pranks, similar to what we do on April 1st, only theirs go from January 1st until the 6th, so you have to stay on your guard. I wanted to get away to listen to some bowl games on the Voice of America, but we had to be sociable and stick around since it was now "coffee time."

One of the issues for a lot of us was the Ecuadorian desire to please, to be sociable, to offer all that they can, even in very humble circumstances, to be accommodating. And they do it in a very insistent manner. To turn them down would be considered rude or insulting. What was offered usually involved something alcoholic. We finally did get away to listen to a game, only to be invited to return for a supper of *cui* (known in the U. S. as guinea pig) and *trago*, which, as I've noted, literally means "drink." When offered in more humble homes it is usually the rot-gut, belly-burning, sugar cane-based alcoholic "shot" that is a staple of dinner, after dinner and evening consumption in all of Ecuador. The guinea pig is served with head and teeth fully intact and, providing you can get by that, it's not too bad if you can convince yourself that it's like eating rabbit. We finally said, "*buenas noches*" at about 9:30 and headed to Ed's for a good night's sleep.

...AND WHILE I WAS OUT

October, November and December, 1963

THE LAST THREE MONTHS OF 1963 HAD SHAKEN MOST OF THE world. Civil unrest continued in the States; the U. S. backed a *coup d'etat* in Vietnam; and assassinations were viewed in real time on television. The nation mourned its leader. Presidents, kings and dignitaries from all over the world came to the United States to express their respect, sympathy and condolences. However, in Ecuador life went on very much as it does in other third world countries where the daily goal for most is to stay alive and endure another day. We Peace Corps Volunteers went on with business as usual as the holidays came and went, and we prepared for our transitions to new assignments. No special ceremonies were planned nor held.

Some of the major events that would change the world while I was out at the time included:

Politics:

- President Kennedy signs the ratification for the Nuclear Test Ban Treaty.
- Kennedy is assassinated during a motorcade in Dallas on November 22nd and America loses its innocence.
- Lyndon Baines Johnson is sworn in on Air Force One in

Dallas before returning to Washington and the country is put on high alert.
- Jack Ruby shoots and kills Lee Harvey Oswald and the event is seen on live television.
- Kennedy's funeral is beamed around for all the world to see wherever there were television sets.
- The Warren Commission is established to investigate the assassination.

Vietnam:

- 225,000 students in Chicago boycott schools in a "Freedom Day Protest."
- Conscientious objector, Eugene Keyes, burns his draft card in Champaign, Illinois. It is the first well-publicized incident of draft card burning.
- President Diem of South Vietnam is overthrown and assassinated by members of the South Vietnamese Army in a U. S. backed *coup d'etat.*

International:

- West and East Berlin German authorities sign an agreement allowing for transit from West to East Berlin.
- The first crack appears in the Iron Curtain as the Berlin wall opens for the first time to West Berliners.

Culture:

- The Beatles sign a three-show contract to appear on the Ed Sullivan Show.

THE END OF INTERREGNUM

I MIGHT HAVE CALLED THIS PERIOD "INTERMISSION," AS IN between missions or assignments, but the mission went on. The "higher ups" in the school construction effort (Watson, Baird, Ruilloba, Justo Andrade and others) were still meeting with principals of the committees in the towns and villages where schools were to be built, working out final details of which we were not informed nor aware. If anything was an intermission, it was the last couple of weeks when we celebrated Christmas and went on our various mini-vacations. It was a time of transition and, for me, it was a time to set up a base in the city of Loja. It was nice to have a place of respite, a place to go to commune and commiserate with other Volunteers, to speak English and vent about the people, policies, practices and prejudices we encountered out in our respective communities.

I came down on the bus from Ed's place in Cuenca on January 3rd and stayed with Bill Fizetti, who was working with a Peace Corps group centered around the Heifer Project. After picking up a bundle of letters and audio tapes from the post office, I spent a lot of time catching up on them and returning the favor. The audio tapes were a device that Ann and I had employed to hear each other's voice and give a better sense of connection and intensity to our thoughts. They were recorded on a battery driven Aiwa TP 50 plastic tape recorder that created some laughs from time to time as the speed was dependent on the power of the batteries which were never in complete sync. I made a recording singing, "I'll be Home for Christmas," and it came out sounding like a funeral dirge.

Gerry, the volunteer with whom I had shared the event filled bus trip to Quito, was to be stationed in Loja. In the next couple of days, I went with him to rent a third-floor room over the newest store in town. It was to be his place, but Joe and I pitched in on the rent in order to have somewhere to store some of the clothes and things we would not need at our assigned locations. It was also good to have a place to stay when we came in to Loja on trips to meet with the Ecuadorian paymaster on the school construction and to purchase supplies not available in La Toma. The room was all fresh lumber so we spent time sweeping it out and applying an oil-based stain to the floor. We purchased a table and four chairs from the local jail (which they apparently made instead of license plates) and, with the addition of the purchase of some plumbing pipes to make a clothes rack, we were in business. The rest of the amenities would be up to Gerry.

John Smith and Doc Caplin rolled into town unannounced. I received a TB shot from the Doc, and Smith informed me that I would be traveling with Ruilloba, the School Construction Chief Engineer, to visit a number of projects in progress throughout the Province of Loja. We left the next day and drove from Loja to Macará, a town on the border with Peru. The scenery was beautiful, but the roads were terrible. The Pan-American Highway was under construction on the leg from Loja to Catamayo/La Toma and that was bad enough, with detours and major drop offs down the side of the mountainous route. Once one left the Pan-Am route, which we did in Catamayo, most of the roads were torturous driving. In Macará, down near the Peruvian border, I had the chance to catch up with two Volunteers, Carmelo Cruz and Phil Button, guys I had not seen for, what seemed like, ages. We visited their construction site, caught up and compared notes and stories.

The next day, as we drove to Celica, I had the chance to drive for the first time in two and a half months. It was a good feeling, but our vehicle was a Forward Control or cab over engine Jeep. With the roads as they were, it was more than a little unsettling to be hanging over the front end of the wheels with no hood in front of you on curving, rutted roads. I finally had to give up the wheel as we got off the twisting and turning main road and on to an even worse road. It took us to Celica and a little village called Pindal, even further back in the mountains where the school was located.

The following day was a long grind. We left Pindal at 7:20 a.m. and drove all the way to my old haunts high up in the mountains, Cangonamá. It was nice to see that they were making good progress. After a brief visit there, we headed back to Loja where we arrived at 2:00 in the morning. In the three days we had covered 411 miles of tough mountainous roads and trails, some of which I had driven.

I gained tremendous respect for Engineer Ruilloba, this dedicated, hard-working and equally hard driving individual. As I said before, he was hard to pinpoint. He came across as very tough on the carpenters, and yet he really cared about the program. He was the ramrod, the foreman, who had to ensure that the jobs were being done to the level of quality required and that they were being done on schedule. Both objectives were subject to the training, experience and skill levels of the local workers assigned, as well as the supply lines of pay and materials to the sites. To say that both areas often left something to be desired is an understatement. I had a lot of sympathy for Ruilloba which would as time went on turn into empathy after a few months on the job in Catamayo.

PART III

ON MY OWN

BY JANUARY 11, 1964, I HAD PACKED UP THE THINGS I WAS PLANNING on taking to my new assignment in Catamayo, which the locals usually referred to as "La Toma." The name came from a large hacienda that existed where water "was taken" from the Catamayo river and used for irrigation. Literally *la toma* means "the taking" and the name stuck. I don't know which came first but, frankly, La Toma was a lot easier for me to say (and type!) than Catamayo. To this day, the lower valley of the area is the home to the Monterrey Sugar Processing Mill and still uses irrigation to grow and process cane sugar. Much of that sugar cane in my days there was then used to make the ("dreaded" for me) drink, "Puro Lojano," the brand name for the "*trago*" with which I was soon to become all too familiar.

I learned much later than I should have that La Toma is virtually set in the middle of four or five *haciendas* (plantations/estates). The *estancierios* (ranchers/farmers), owners of the fertile lower part of the valley, including the sugar mill, are also the owners of much of the dry upper part of the valley in which most of the *barrios* (neighborhoods) lie. Thus, the residents of the *barrios* owe more allegiance to them than they do to the town.

They live on, and most work on, the property of the *haciendas.* The idea of patronism is ingrained here. The feeling that if any improvements come, they'll come from the *patrón,* the owner of the land, not from one's own efforts. That mentality is one that any Peace Corps Volunteer had to work hard to overcome to get help from the *mingas* and for any other community development work to be done.

The town of La Toma was located in the largest and most fertile valley in the Province of Loja. It lies about eleven miles from Loja, as the crow flies, and about twenty-five miles of winding, curvy, precipitous road by vehicle. For me the vehicle was usually a rickety bus or, if I was lucky enough to catch a ride, a Peace Corps Jeep or a Toyota truck. The ride was always made even more adventurous because the way was often blocked by the Caterpillar bulldozers, scrapers, and workers I've referenced, busily making improvements to the Pan-American Highway on which both Loja and La Toma lay.

When I write about the "highway" it is in name only. At that point in time, it was a highway in the sense that it was graded and wider than most other roads in the country. The blasting away of the mountainsides made its switchback curves a little less dangerous than the narrow, sharp curves that previously existed, and the fact that it had a gravel base meant it was navigable in almost all kinds of weather. There were no guardrails, and that always made for an exciting ride.

When I use the term "fertile valley," perhaps you picture a lush green tropical area with lots of trees and tall grass and cultivated fields as far as the eye can see. And, indeed, much of the valley looked that way - about four miles south and west of the town. The town itself looked more like something out of a setting for a Western movie. It was one of the few Ecuadorian towns without a town square of some kind. The square, *la plaza,* was there, but there was nothing in it except dust and, from time to time, a few wandering pigs. The following is how I described the place in a letter home to my folks:

> Let me take you on a tour of La Toma. As the bus descends down the mountain on the ride from Loja, we enter the town. On the right are a number of one and two-story buildings. Some of the one-story buildings are all adobe with slanting, clay tiled porches in front, held up by whatever wooden poles are available. While others, both one-story and two-story buildings, have painted stucco facades in white, pink and/or green hues. They are usually topped off with uncolored clay tiles, but a few of the newer ones have painted tiles. These buildings are mostly storefronts of some sort, a hotel, a few walled residences and the town bus stop. This stretch is about half a football field in length. On the left, across the barren square, the prominent façade of the Catholic church looms large. Its tower contains a bell as well as a loudspeaker. The church is covered in smooth, grey stucco with large, unadorned, double wooden doors at the entrance. Connected to the church is a long, dark green building that houses a parochial school that runs almost the full length of that leg of the square. At the end is a white two-story building with a balcony that overlooks the square. As our bus arrives at the end of the "first leg," a choice must be made. To go straight takes us past some smaller, nondescript humble dwellings and businesses and continues sloping down, past the cane fields and on to San Pedro, the next town of any size, which lies eleven miles away to the west. But if our bus turns left, we take the other leg of the square that leads to the airport which serves Loja and accounts for most of the prosperity and activity in the town. At the corner is a little one-story restaurant with a tile covered porch named 'Noches de Rhonda.' Beyond that restaurant, down the second leg of our *plaza,* are

a series of *tiendas* (stores) along a covered walkway consisting of a shoe repair shop, feed goods, produce, and something approaching a bar or hangout where a number of individuals gather. All we need now are a couple of posts to tie up a horse and we can shoot our first movie scene.

Beyond the main square are a number of adobe residences and dry, dusty "streets," pathways mostly, that run up to the foothills of the barren Andes Mountains, which surround the valley and town on the east, north and west sides. If there were ever trees on them, they would have been cut down hundreds of years before. In spite of the fact that two rivers run through the valley down below, the town itself is almost desertlike, similar to areas in New Mexico or Arizona. Here live the families, many in homes without running water or electricity: the people who work the cane fields, feed the cane mills, do the labor, work the stores and raise their families. These people are the folks I am now eager to meet and, hopefully, engage in improving their lot in life in any way I can. And this ends our tour which I hope has provided some flavor of the place.

I was a little apprehensive about being on my own, of course. My Spanish was improving, and I had picked up on a number of Ecuadorian colloquialisms along the way, but there would be no back-up. No Joe Orr nor Doug Strauss to jump in if my mental hunt for the proper Spanish word failed. But I was as ready as I would ever be. Time to jump into the deep end of the pool and start swimming.

Having been promised a ride with Justo Andrade to get to our orientation meeting with the committee in La Toma, I gathered all the things I thought would be necessary to establish an initial

The main street of La Toma, with the Noches de Ronda (Suco's) Restaurant sign on the left. Gravel on the road is in preparation for improvement to the Pan-American Highway that runs through the town.

dwelling there. Saturday, January 11, 1964, was my official introduction to La Toma. Justo told me that we would take a different car because of all the people that were going and that I would have to take all my things in the next day or two. We left and drove the twenty-five miles in fairly good time and had our initial meeting with the members of the school construction committee. A number of the local teachers were in attendance as well.

Also at the meeting was a man who seemed to be at the center of all that happened, Father Eliseo Arias Carrión. Padre Arias, as he was known, was a very influential member of the School Construction Committee. The committee's job was to raise the local contributions of money, materials and support; handle the paperwork; do the contracting for the project; and create some enthusiasm when *mingas* were required. Padre Arias was a short, rather rotund individual, slightly balding and looked a little like Friar Tuck in his black cassock. Effusive and displaying a great sense of humor, he put me at ease with his warm welcome. Justo explained my role to them as that of a coordinator and supervisor but most of all as a friend and helper for whatever they wanted me to do. He introduced me as "full of vigor, enthusiastic and 'here with an ideal'."

Over lunch with Padre Arias and some others, we discussed the progress on the construction which was already underway and the plans for the future. After we finished eating, I was informed that a room had been selected for me at a rooming house close to the center of town. Given our experience in Cangonamá, I thought I had better check it out.

The room was in a whitewashed two-story building, with a balcony in the center overlooking the path of the Pan-Am Highway, which it fronted. It was the type of place where the family that owns the property also lives and rents out individual rooms, usually on a long-term basis. The windowless rooms faced and formed a small courtyard in the center of the building, following the customary construction practices in much of Latin America. After lunch, at around three o'clock, I went over to see the room that was on the second floor. It was small and clean. Small, about ten feet by twelve feet, but adequate for my needs. It contained no lights nor electrical outlets nor any sign of plumbing but it did have a small table, a chair and a bed. The folks there explained that there were facilities down the hall and that they would supply me with a washbasin and pitcher. (Shades of 1900.) However, with the addition of a few amenities, such as my Peace Corps stove, Coleman lanterns and some additional furniture, I figured it would serve my minimal needs quite well.

My "home" in La Toma, a windowless room in the upper right side of the building. Downstairs neighbor, Carlos García, looks over the shared upstairs balcony.

I returned to the church office and one of the school teachers, Marlene (mar-lay-nay) Bermeo, a cute, petite young lady who had been at the Padre's office when we met, handed me the coat I had left behind. Honest, I was not like the woman who drops her handkerchief in the hopes of being noticed, although it was nice to be noticed by a pretty girl. Justo, Padre Arias and I left the church, joined by the Provincial Minister of Education and two other men from the Department of Education, to visit a school in a nearby hamlet set way back in the foothills, called El Tumbo. (Aptly named, it translates as "the shock" or "the jolt.") It was a humble little place, but full of enthusiasm for the occasion.

There was, of course, a welcoming committee complete with the obligatory shots of the nasty Puro Lojano, the local commercial *trago*. At least Puro Lojano came in a bottle that actually had a label and a seal on it. Much of what was available, I have no doubt, was local brew. There were flowery speeches and a program presented by the students, much like programs of kids in grades first through sixth anywhere, but with the addition of the playing of wooden flutes and simple drums. Justo and the Minister of Education were presented with medals; we had dinner and more Puro Lojano; and then headed back to Loja. I decided that I was going to like La Toma. The people seemed very nice; the Padre was great fun; and Engineer Ruilloba told me that that *Maestro* Illescas, the lead carpenter, was one of the best in the program.

I spent the following Monday morning getting my things ready, bought a few additional items I decided I would need, and packed up the Peace Corps Jeep which I requested to use for the day. *Maestro* Illescas was in Loja so I offered to take him back. When I arrived, ready to move in to my room, I discovered that the owners were going to paint the room for me so I put all that I had carried in into another room and left again for Loja. The plan was for me to come back with Mario Mena, so he could pay the workers.

For lack of a better title, Mario was the paymaster for the School Construction Cooperative, and he was a piece of work. He was a thin, slight man in his mid-30's, almost always dressed in a suit, often with a vest, and eager to let you know he had been to school. His card and stationery carried the title *"licenciado,"* meaning that he was a graduate. In a country where most of the population at the time only went through sixth grade, that was an accomplishment. However, he seemed to carry himself as if he had a law degree. He was always cordial with a nice smile, always saying he was willing to accommodate - however seldom doing so, and always late. He was not alone in that.

One thing we all learned very early in the country is that the concept which we so value in the U. S. of being on time, promptness, time management, etc., did not exist in Ecuador. We were warned of it in training, but experiencing it was another thing. They employed the phrase *"ya mismo"* which literally translates as "right now." But it could mean "right now," "any minute," "pretty soon," "eventually," or "in the next few days." It was maddening to ask when something or somebody was going to arrive and hear in response *"ya mismo!"* And when someone did arrive you could never expect an apology for their lateness. It was just "business as usual."

I spent the next day in Loja waiting for Mario to show up. While I was waiting, I helped Joe and Gerry get the apartment we shared into better shape by putting up shelves and adding a few other touches to make it look like "home." I finally went to pick up Mario in the Peace Corps Jeep along with another Volunteer who was to bring it back from La Toma. When we got to Mena's place, he said he just couldn't make it that day. I had returned just to transport him, spent most of the day waiting for him, and lost the time I could have been fixing up my room. When I got to La Toma, I endured the *maestro's* justifiable anger when I informed him that he wouldn't be paid this day. (Just as he and the workers had not been paid for the last month and a half.) I didn't know the details of the "why" of all that, but a lot of my money would have been on Mario Mena. I sensed that maybe, there was some "Trouble in River City," and that I would have to learn more about it.

When I got to my room, I discovered the owners had painted it a "lovely" baby pink and pastel green. But they had also threaded an electric cord in over the doorway, so I now would have at least a little light. I found out two teachers also lived there: Luis García, with his wife and two children; and Carlos Carrión, the son of the owner, and his family. They came up to help me move in, motivated more (I suspect) by curiosity than altruism. They dug into and asked about everything I took out of my footlocker, admiring and asking about things and wanting to know the value of each: the 35 mm camera, the Zenith Trans-Oceanic radio, the hand cranked movie camera, the tape recorder, and the like. Not wanting to sound like the rich guy from the "great warehouse to the North," I told them I couldn't recall the price of most and that many had been gifted to me.

Now I was a monk. I had my bed, a table, a chair and a wash basin to start me off. I decided to use the now empty footlocker as a dresser until I could get one built or bought. So, after unpacking and arranging everything I could, I went out for one beer with Luis, came back and sacked out at about 11:00. I was truly on my own.

GETTING TO KNOW YOU

FOR THE NEXT FEW WEEKS, I PROBABLY LOOKED LIKE THE BALL in a handball court. I was bouncing all over the town, full of energy, eager to please, eager to know who was who, what they wanted to do, what I could do to help make that happen. The song, "Getting to Know You," from the musical *The King and I* describes the scene pretty well: *"Getting to know you, getting to know all about you; getting to like you, getting to hope you like me... You are precisely my cup of tea."* I had the feeling that La Toma was "My cup of tea," and I wanted to know all about it.

In the first few weeks, I met with a number of people. The first person, and the one who became my most ardent supporter, was the treasurer of the school construction committee. His name was German Coronel but everyone called him "Suco" (sue-co). In Quechua, the indigenous language, *suco* means "white" or "blond," and he was usually called Suco Candela, "white candle." In addition to being very light skinned, he also had red hair. Suco owned and ran the corner restaurant that hung out the "Noches de Rhonda" sign. He employed a weekly meal ticket system, a small card with boxes to be checked off for breakfast, lunch or dinner with each use. I quickly signed up for one of these tickets, and the restaurant became my place of refuge and some solace when things got tough. Suco could always cheer me up when I was depressed or calm me down when angry (or "*muy bravo*" as Suco would say).

He and I talked about doing a public latrine project using a Cinva-Ram machine, a manual device that we had used in training to make compressed bricks of sand, clay and a little cement. It created a sort of modern-day adobe brick that looked better and lasted longer than the original product. He also thought it might be used to build a permanent building for their cultural center which was a sort of multi-purpose community building. After talking with Suco, I wrote a letter to James Watson asking him if we could have a Cinva-Ram device sent down and described its potential uses.

The *Jefe de Rurales* (Chief of Police) came by Suco's one evening early on and said he was glad to meet me because he said he had heard that I was "very enthusiastic." He invited me to come and visit him because he also had some things in mind that he wanted to talk over with me. While meeting with him and other folks, I heard support for the latrine project from a number of people. Still others mentioned a public playground, a library, and a youth center. There were three adult centers but none for the kids. More than once I heard, "Maybe you could teach an English class."

As I settled in, my "getting to know you" included meeting locals who helped me with furnishing my room. A businessman and committee member offered me a table, which I gladly accepted. I put the Coleman stove on that along with a five-gallon water jug and built a shelf to hold the pots and pans, and other items that constituted "my kitchen." The stove was used primarily to boil the water, which I did faithfully, adding a couple of iodine pills, as always, to top off the purification process. (I was glad to hear that Suco also boiled whatever water he used at the restaurant, which is one of the reasons I felt comfortable eating there on a regular basis.) I decorated the room with big maps of Ecuador on one wall and the U. S. on another. I put up some pictures from "home." Somewhere along the way, I was also given a small dresser and a mirror. My footlocker, with the addition of a rolled-up sleeping bag on top, became a seat for guests.

I got into sort of a routine of eating breakfast at Suco's, going over to the school construction site and working from 8:30 to about 11:00 or 11:30, and then having lunch. I don't believe that all Volunteers pitched in the way I did. In my way of thinking, working along with these people served three primary purposes. The first was to demonstrate that the *Norte Americanos* were not prejudiced nor above getting their hands dirty. The second was to act as a role model for the middle class, the businessmen and others, so that when it came time for doing the "*mingas*," those bucket brigade-like community efforts, when rocks, sand and or gravel needed to be gathered or cement poured, they would feel free to pitch in. The third purpose was to be a bit of a quality control guy, not so much with this group regarding the work, (they were good at what they did) but to put a watchful eye on the supply lines of rebar steel, cement and bricks. We had to go to Mario Mena to get those materials delivered on time and that could be a problem. (Incidentally, Mario showed up three days after he was originally scheduled to pay the workers on that last go around.)

Remember that I was in the Southern Hemisphere. In January it was the middle of summer, and the heat could get oppressive. I quickly learned that I needed something to ward off the sun, so I purchased a Panama hat in a local store. It was still in its raw form: unblocked and untrimmed on the brim, but I thought it served the purpose, and I liked the effect. In reality, the Panama hat is a product of Ecuador, made with Ecuadorian straw, woven tightly under water, processed, trimmed, sometimes colored, and then shipped out for sale. Early travelers through the Panama Canal would purchase the product and the name "Panama hat" stuck. My standard uniform of the day was blue jeans, a beige work shirt, solid pair of work boots and my "very dapper" hat.

In the early afternoons I would respond to letters that came in big batches from Ann and in ones and twos from high school and college schoolmates; read a little; or tend to construction related paperwork. Also, I was not beyond grabbing a quick nap in the afternoon which was partially a need for rest and partly escapism, not having to deal with anybody who didn't speak English. Then around 3:00 or so I would return to the worksite to do whatever was needed; check on what I could do for *Maestro* Illescas in terms of communicating with Mario Mena; or go into Loja to bring something out. That was the daily pattern of my work for most days.

Evenings would generally start with dinner at Suco's, and then I had a choice of returning to my room with its forty to sixty-watt bulb's worth of light depending on how much power the town generator was cranking out. If it was too low, I would supplement it with my Coleman lantern and read, do more correspondence or write in my journal. Or usually, especially in the early days, someone would come up and invite me out for a drink or some other activity, too many of which involved those shot glasses of Puro Lojano. I could have said, "No," to those shots, and I often did. But when I did so, I risked offending them because that was all they could afford. Often, I would suggest beer and pay for a round or two depending on the size the group, which was always just the men. But they generally could not afford that luxury, and another bottle of Puro Lojano would hit the table.

One of the dryer outings I had in the first couple of weeks was an invitation to go out to the local pool hall with my neighbors, Luis and Carlos. Since I was far from being familiar with their approach to the table and not much of a player myself, I taught them the only thing I knew, our system of eight-ball pool. They had never seen it before and really ate it up. Of course, being old pool sharks, they were much better at it than I. The real pay-off to this effort was that it was a good way to "bond," at least with Carlos and Luis, and I think it really paid off.

It paid off so well, in fact, Carlos came up a few nights later to invite me out again for another round. This outing led to a definitely non-dry experience. The round of pool lasted until 11:00 that night with Carlos showing two other teachers how to play and enjoy it. Then three more male teachers showed up and joined in. This group then invited me out for some Puro Lojano. I said, "No," to that and suggested beer, which we drank until someone ordered two bottles of that rot gut. This was good example of what I described before, the night led to a good and well-lubricated idea generating session, much of which never came to fruition. However, the time and effort brought me some acceptance, respect and support down the line. "Drinking in the line of duty," I decided, "must be the way to get things done in La Toma." I never made that connection consciously, but that seemed to be the *modus operandi* of the place.

Part of the bouncing around in my "getting to know you" phase included an invitation to join Luis Garcia and his family in a swim at our landlord's home which was a fairly spacious place with a swimming pool down in the lush, green part of the valley. I gathered that our landlord was doing quite well at whatever it was that he did and surmised that Luis' wife was probably the owner's daughter. Marlene, the teacher I had met at the Padre's office, was also there and was apparently a cousin of Luis. In retrospect, there were a lot of connections of which I was unaware at the time. The Padre just used the designation "Arias" and not the "Carrion" in everyday interactions. Carlos Carrion was the owner's son as I mentioned, and I found out much later that the hotel near the bus stop was owned by the Padre's mother. With all these family ties, I was probably being watched closely, and my activities relayed on a regular basis to the good Padre who tended to keep tabs on all that went on in his parish. The good news about the trip to the pool was that I was able to get my first hot shower since arriving. The only amenity at the boarding house was an outside shower head that offered only cold water.

In addition to including me in a family outing, Luis introduced me to the local Director of Education and together we went over to the girls' school. While there, I got talked into agreeing to teach some plays to their girls' basketball team. (After all, I was the star bench seater - after fouling out - on my high school basketball team.) I added that to my list of projects, which was about to get even longer.

My network of acquaintances kept expanding. I also met with some of the guys from the Guarderas Construction Company who were working on the Pan-Am Highway and living locally. They were the truck drivers, grader operators and other machinery operators, and a pretty savvy group they were. Many of them were ex-military and, therefore, had some exposure to Americans as a result. One of them, a sharp young guy named Juvenal Galarga, had connections with the local military contingent that had a barracks near the airport. He was very interested in U. S. culture and nagged me in a persistent way to start an English class. Knowledge of English was seen as a "ticket to ride," the "get out of jail free card" for a lot of people. He was not the only person interested. The teachers and a couple of the regulars at Suco's said they were interested as well.

I was told by one of the Peace Corps Area Reps who had stopped by shortly after I arrived that there had been a previous Volunteer in La Toma for about two or three months, but I should forget he ever existed. The Area Rep said that it seemed that he had screwed up everything he touched, and the Heifer Project

Volunteer who accompanied the Rep confirmed the story. Later on, I talked to some Volunteers who knew him and may have been some of his drinking buddies. They didn't think he was so bad, but they could not name a thing he had accomplished. The good news seemed to be that he would not be a tough act to follow. I sure hoped that I could improve on the image he left behind. One thing I did hear about him was that he had attempted to teach an English class. However, they felt his command of Spanish was so bad that effort had also fizzled.

After much thought, I decided that one high impact thing I could do, and do well, was to teach an English class to the folks who had expressed an interest. After all, my mother was a high school English teacher.... All I needed was a place to hold the classes and some basic text books which I could procure from the Peace Corps offices. I would talk to Padre Arias about the possibility of using one of the rooms in the parochial school in the evening. And therein lies a tale and what just about became the bane of my existence in the first couple of months.

APRENDAMOS INGLES!

THE SATURDAY AFTER I CHECKED ON THE POURED CONCRETE slabs for the latrine project, I returned to La Toma with the intention of talking to Padre Arias about teaching the English class in one of the rooms at the church school. When I arrived at around 5:00, I discovered that there was a party going on in the courtyard downstairs from my room, and all were well on their way to being totally drunk. I tried to slip out to see the priest, but to accomplish my escape I had to pass through the throng of people below. Someone grabbed me by the arm and "invited" me to have "*uno no mas*" (just one). Well, *uno no mas* turned into about five or six shots of the local Puro rot gut. I finally got out of there well on my way and headed over to see the padre. When I got to the church there were two men from Loja with him, and they were pretty smashed as well. (Did I miss a memo about a national holiday or was this just a normal Saturday night?) One man was the head of Radio Loja and the other was his assistant. They immediately "required" me to join in their imbibing with one of those, "Oh, you don't want to drink with me, eh?" approaches. So, I did, much to my regret the next day. I babbled on about all the problems the Peace Corps Volunteers were having in Loja and probably offended them in the process, but my suspicion is they were probably too far gone to remember it the next day. I did manage to get in my request for a classroom and got Padre Arias' permission to use it. We agreed we would start on Monday night. I left in a fog planning to get something to eat at Suco's in the hopes that some food would sober me up, but Puro had won the day. I headed home and crashed.

Based on my discussions with those who had expressed a desire to learn English, I calculated that we would have about fifteen to twenty people in the class. You may remember that I mentioned a loudspeaker in the bell tower of the church? That's what Padre Arias used to make announcements to the general public. As I was calmly eating my dinner at Suco's on Sunday night I heard this pronouncement floating out over the airways in the plaza: "Our friend and colleague from the United States, who is helping in the construction and supervision of our grand new school, has now offered his services to give free English classes to all those who are interested." I about choked on my soup.

At the appointed time on Monday night, no less than ninety people arrived to sign up for class. They ranged in age from ten years old to very old, and one person there was leaving for the United States the following week. Many had never even finished the sixth grade, and I'm pretty sure some were not even literate in Spanish. I decided to have them fill out their names on a list (or sign with an X). I took the list to Padre Arias, and we decided to eliminate anyone who hadn't finished the sixth grade and those under sixteen years of age. That at least whittled the number down to forty-one men and fifteen women. The room would not accommodate that number so I decided to have a beginners' class from 7:00 to 8:00 and then another for those that knew or thought they knew a little English from 8:00 to 9:00. What had started out as a nice gesture was about to turn into a major task.

When we got back home Luis took me aside and suggested that to avoid criticism, I should probably have all females in the first class where there would be more supervision. I thought, "Yeah, and maybe I could run four sessions a night!" I decided I would stick with our first plan (beginners and those with some exposure) and challenge the cultural norms a bit. I figured if the men couldn't be gentlemen for at least an hour there wasn't much hope for them. The Feminine Mystique, published in February of 1963, may have been changing things in the U. S., but in very Catholic Ecuador, the separation of the sexes in classrooms was still very much in vogue.

As with most Latin American countries, Ecuador reflected the machismo culture of the era, which I suspect continues to this day, though perhaps in more subtle form. It was not subtle at all in the sixties. It is reflected in a strong sense of male pride, whether it is deserved or not. It often comes out in the form of boasting, bluster, swagger, irreverence and often brutish behavior which I witnessed often in some of the La Toma population. It's the sense that one perceives himself as "God's gift to women," no matter his looks, condition or behavior. Males conduct themselves in a superior manner to anyone they perceive as inferior, which means women (sometimes even their wives) and anyone of lesser economic or ethnic status.

I eventually succumbed to the local pressure to separate the females from the males. Given some of the rowdy and childish behavior I endured for the first few weeks of the class, I was glad to do it and, as it turned out, it worked much better all around. This *gringo* had learned that sometimes it is better to "do as the Romans do." I split the first class into two groups, the women from 7:00 to 7:30 and the men from 7:30 to 8:00. This allowed for much more individual attention. More importantly for the good of the "mores" of the community, it allowed the ladies to leave and go home without the danger of being bothered by the males doing what many of these males were prone to do. They didn't physically harass the women but were not beyond making crude and suggestive comments.

Prior to the division of the sexes, I had decided to use a book called *Aprendamos Inglés* (We Learn English) that was in our Peace Corps footlocker and written especially for teaching English as a foreign language. I planned to introduce the sounds and articulation of the vowels and consonants and planned on using phonetics. Sweating profusely and wondering what the hell I'd gotten myself into, I launched into my teaching, which was mostly the class repeating the sounds I was demonstrating. They were a pretty unruly bunch, talking too much and jostling each other like children would do. That got me through the first class, and I sincerely hoped I had driven some away with that approach. The second class had about twenty people in it and that went fairly well using the same approach.

On the second class night a number of people showed up who hadn't gotten the message on Sunday or had heard about the class by word of mouth. I had about sixty people packed into the little room. I explained what the requirements were: sixth grade grads and over sixteen years old. This culled out a few. However, most stuck around out of curiosity and the fact that there was probably nothing else for them to do. The next night the numbers were down a bit in the first class, but the unruly behavior continued and slowed up the process.

My days were getting pretty full now, working at the school by day, some class prep during the lunch break along with my usual activities, then a quick dinner, and teaching each night. As the classes dwindled a bit more to about a total of seventy, I asked how many people would buy a book to use in class, as I had milked the sounds, intonation and accents approach about as far as I could. It was time for the real thing, the: "Hello my name is ______. How are you?" and "Where is the train station?" phase, including vocabulary and everyday phrases. Almost all the hands went up and I ordered fifty books. On one of my trips into Loja I purchased a receipt book so I could keep track of who paid and give folks a receipt. The following night, I decided to use the class time to collect money for the books and write out receipts, so I didn't prepare anything for that hour. Out of all the hands that had eagerly gone up, I sold a total of seventeen books in about twenty minutes. So, I attempted to fill up the next forty minutes "tap dancing" my way along and repeating much of what we had done the past few nights. It was a mess. Fortunately, the second class, which consisted mostly of teachers in the town and a few Guarderas Pan-Am Highway construction guys, went well and redeemed my evening.

In early February I decided to see how the classes were coming along (my impression was not so well.) I did two nights of review and decided to type up a test. I did it one afternoon, after buying some paper in Loja so I could pass out a test to each individual. The day the test was to be given, I worked on it for a couple of hours (test writing not being my "long suit"), and at about 4:30 I finished and went to the church to see if I could use the padre's (now archaic) mimeograph machine. He explained that he was just leaving and had to lock up the office, but he so graciously gave me a piece of carbon paper. (Also archaic.) One piece of carbon paper! Given the time available I knew I was not going to be able to type up enough copies and wasn't even sure that this piece of carbon paper would handle that many. I decided to just make twenty for the second class.

By 6:30 I had finished that task and, not having had supper, I headed over to the classroom and decided to improvise for the first class and write the test questions on two sides of the small, wobbly, portable blackboard in the room. The door was locked and with the Padre gone, I finally found someone who had enough authority to get the key and open the door. It was now 6:45 and the class was set to start at 7:00. I asked the gathering crowd of students to stay outside while I took twenty minutes to write up the test questions on the board. As I opened the door to let the students in, I was immediately hit with a water balloon and a second flew by me and hit the blackboard, erasing more than half of what was on one side. This was someone anticipating *Carnaval,* which was just around the corner, similar to people setting off firecrackers before the Fourth of July. The fact that I had a horrendous cold didn't help matters. I became, as Suco would say, "*muy bravo*!" Dragging from a cold; having spent the last four and a half hours getting ready for this evening; and skipping dinner in the process, I read them the riot act. Hardly cowed by my ranting, they finally dropped their ammunition and came into the classroom, giggling and shoving each other, wondering why their "*profesor*" had no sense of humor.

I handed out the paper on which they were to write their answers. I then gave them the instructions to write down the number of each question on the board and put their answer to that question behind the number. I got them started and, while I worked to reconstruct the questions on the side of the board that had been hit, they talked and cheated and copied answers from one another. I mentally threw up my hands and waited for them to hand in their papers. Two things were readily apparent. Number one, they hadn't understood the instructions. Number two, most had apparently neither learned nor retained, a damn thing in the last two weeks. The results in the second class were much better, and I felt somewhat more confident regarding my teaching prowess. If both groups had bombed, I would had have needed to look hard at the premise, "If the student hasn't learned, the teacher hasn't taught." I had done okay and, with some modifications, the first class of fifty dwindled down over time to a hard core of people who were never particularly good but very loyal and eager to try. I made some friends there at least, and the members of the second class, admittedly, became my "teacher's pets" as we worked toward completing the book.

CARNAVAL!

As a travel brochure said, "*Carnaval marks the passage from the darkness of Winter to the blossoms, fruits and fertility of Spring. It is Latin America's version of Mardi Gras. Carnaval in Ecuador is like none other in Latin America. In this very Catholic country, it celebrates excess in abundance in the days leading up to 'Fat Tuesday,' the day before Lent begins.*" Every city has its own customs, but the key word I take from that brochure's description is "excess." It includes some customs borrowed from a Quechua holiday celebrating the moon, in which water and flour were used as symbols. Ecuadorians throw water at each other in any form they can find (water balloons, buckets or hoses are all fair game) followed by showers of flour or corn starch. It is a national holiday that includes parades, dances, drinking, and partying - lots of drinking and partying. And La Toma certainly did its part in fine fashion.

The *maestro* and his crew took the week off and headed to their homes in Otavalo for the holidays. Given what I had heard of the festivities that were planned, I cancelled classes for the week of *Carnaval*. I figured I would have a week of rest and relaxation and maybe get rid of my cold. I was mistaken.

Of course, no *Carnaval* would be complete without a queen, and La Toma was no exception. A spirted campaign was held the week before *Carnaval* started. A number of local civic societies sponsored candidates. As a "local celebrity" I was asked to be in on the official counting of ballots. One of the teachers told me that the selection process would go on until 8:00, so I asked Padre Arias to cancel the evening's classes during his announcements. As it turned out, I just stood around while everyone else counted. When I tried to get in on the process, they wanted to do it by themselves. I was at least asked to put my signature on a piece of paper saying how much money had been raised, as people voted with contributions of money. I also certified that the winner was Cecilia Murillo, a pretty young neighbor, whom I didn't really know except by sight. The whole process was finished by 6:00 p.m. When I went to eat, at around 7:00, I found out that there were about forty confused people, who apparently had not heard the cancellation announcement, waiting at the school for class to start. So, having made up my mind to get some rest because my cold was killing me, I gave them the news and headed home to do just that.

Just as I laid down, Carlos and some of the other teachers showed up, wanting to drag me out for a Puro or two to celebrate the selection of our neighbor as *Carnaval* Queen. (If she hadn't won, I've no doubt it would have been to mourn her loss.) You know my opinion of Puro by now, so I tried to politely decline using the cold as my defense. As usual they weren't having it. Finally, to get them off my back and out of my room, I went. They were having nothing to do with beer that night. It turned into another *trago*-filled bout, with Carlos regaling me with the history and injustice of what Peru had done in the Frontier War of 1943 and offering me half his library to do research on the subject. I stumbled out of there at about 11:00 and never heard a word about the border war from him again.

A week later there was a parade with some of the Guarderas trucks serving as floats, a few cars decorated with flowers, one carrying Queen Cecilia, and a "four-note" grade school drum and bugle unit marching along to the heavy beat of the drums. They were followed by contingents of people in colorful outfits from the various civic groups and clubs. Then it was time for the Queen's Coronation, the presentation and decorations reminiscent of what you might see at an eighth-grade prom. This was followed by the Grand Ball which was held at the local outdoor basketball court with a band that even the locals said "stunk." I stayed for the coronation ceremonies but snuck out and tried to get some rest. However, some of the teachers, "thinking of my better interests" came and dragged me off. This time I managed to avoid "the nasty" and stayed quite sober while watching the deterioration of my fellow celebrants.

The next day *Carnaval* started in earnest. The idea is to soak everyone in sight and hit people in the face and elsewhere with water balloons and then pour flour on your targets while wearing their good clothes. This continues to go on along with the dancing, drinking and partying. Such fun, they think. I thought not.

I managed to avoid all that was going on outside the house until about 1:00 in the afternoon. That's when a Colombian fellow who worked at the sugar mill in the valley showed up. He was a friend of Carlos and was pretty drunk already. He kindly invited me to drive him, his wife and daughter around in his Jeep so I could see what was going on all over town. I agreed to do so. We picked up a couple of Carlos' friends, as well as the teacher, Marlene, and drove out to the military compound near the airport where we stopped. There was a huge water fight going on with some of the military guys. I got soaked in a battle with the base's commander, who had become a good friend by now, and the rest of the gang got thoroughly soaked as well. I drove the group back into town, all of us still soaking wet. We parked the Jeep and were immediately attacked again. We exchanged "fire" with whomever it was (groups roamed the streets), and after about five minutes, I decided the novelty was well worn off and went back to my room to read.

But the "beat went on." That evening Ruben Patiño and Wilson Carrión, Carlos' younger brother, came by and invited me to a party in one of the barrios in the village. Ruben was one of my best students and later became the best friend I had in town among the young guys, but not yet. It wasn't much of a party, and it looked like the "special of the day" was going to be some homemade *trago*. When they started throwing flour and water on me, I said to myself, "The hell with this!" and headed out. I may have offended Ruben, Wilson and the residents of the barrio by doing so, but drinking *trago* in the line of duty had its limits even for me. "Maybe I'm a hardnose," I thought, "but this was not my idea of fun."

Carnaval participants include Ruben Patiño (on left in yellow and blue hat), Carlos Carrión (white T-shirt), Luis García (squatting wearing light shirt and pants) and Miquel Montaño (on far right) winding up to throw another water balloon.

On the way home I ran into one of my students, Pepe Velez, a member of the Guarderas Pan-American Highway construction group. He was just about to invite me in for a beer at Suco's when two very drunk guys who knew Pepe showed up and dragged us both into the restaurant. They began to praise and then condemn the United States and proceeded at great length to provide solutions to all the U. S.-Latin American problems with plans drawn from their vast stores of political knowledge and alcohol. I suffered through about two hours of their yammering in the name of maintaining good international relations and then got the hell out of there. I went home and read Campus Humor in an effort to cheer myself up, at least a little.

The next day was the start of my mini-vacation. I was in my room writing letters when I heard a big commotion outside in the courtyard. It was Carlos with the rest of the gang including Fausto, one of my students, already soaking one another. I decided, "If you can't beat 'em, join 'em." I quickly put on the oldest clothes I had, took off my watch and took out my wallet. Not a moment too soon. In they came and out I went. I was drenched immediately. Having been properly anointed, we all went downstairs. I grabbed a bucket, and we proceeded from house to house soaking everyone in sight. The first stop was at Carlos' cousin's place where Marlene and her very pretty and feisty younger sister, Yolanda, were promptly and thoroughly soaked. They were probably the cutest girls in town and were great sports. This marauding went on until about three or four in the afternoon. That night there was a party at the house that featured - you guessed it - *trago*, Puro Lojano. Followed by anise. Followed by muscatel. By the end of the night my submission (but not conversion) was complete. I was dancing their dances like an old trooper. I had the Latin beat down cold.

I woke up the next morning with my head banging and

thought maybe I could escape all this by grabbing a bus to Loja. But there were no busses running. Apparently, *Carnaval* cancels bus schedules as well. Who knew? As a result, I decided that I would join the family down at *Señor* Carrión's *hacienda* in the valley. I had been invited to attend the previous day as were a number of my English students and other people I knew. It apparently was "the place to be." I got down there at about noon, and the group had already been drinking and soaking each other since 10:00 in the morning. I danced for a bit and then went swimming. The guys started throwing everybody in the pool fully dressed and, of course, as soon as I got dressed again, in I went. This was followed with more drinking and dancing and flour and cornstarch, *ad nauseum*. Such fun? About 6:00 in the evening I decided I had had quite enough and I took off, very glad to see the end of *Carnaval*. Mercifully, Lent was to start the next day.

OUT OF BOUNDS – A TRIP TO ZAMORA

THE NEXT MORNING, I HITCHED A RIDE INTO LOJA WITH ONE OF the guys that had been at the party the day before. When I got to the apartment, I found Joe Orr and Gerry were there along with two other Volunteers, Joe Kelly and Wally Benson. Wally was in from his post in Zamora to pick up a number of items that he arranged to take back with him to the *Oriente*, the lush, verdant, tropical forest of the country where he was assigned. In addition to his school building efforts, he was doing all sorts of innovative projects involving irrigation. He was also a licensed HAM operator and had a lot of experience reaching out to folks all around the world.

I sent off a telegram to Quito ordering the books for the class, and then we all went to dinner. After dinner we saw a movie made in 1955, *To Hell and Back*, playing at the local theater. I hope this gives you some idea of the local offerings, but at least it was in English. It features Audie Murphy, the most decorated soldier of World War II, playing himself and recreating some of his exploits that won him those medals. The movie's soundtrack is filled with patriotic music and was a real grabber that gave me a "proud to be an American" kind of feeling.

After the movie we went back to the apartment and got into one hell of a discussion. You may remember that I said at the outset that Joe Orr was politically savvy. Wally was a well-informed and intelligent engineer, and Joe Kelly was very much on the right of the political spectrum. Given that political science was my major, I figured I was also well prepared to participate. We covered patriotism's impact on Ecuador's history and its people; how its nationalist leaders had gotten them into losing wars with Peru; how and why hearing the Star-Spangled Banner affects us; and pacifism, conscientious objection and civil liberties. We weren't finished yet. We went on to a discussion of liberties in general and one's freedom of action based on one's own principles, values and motivation. We talked far into the night. I marveled at how refreshing it was to be with "the guys," watching a movie in English and having a truly intelligent, sensible discussion after so many nights of Puro driven nonsense.

The last part of our discussion about freedom of action and individual liberty touched on something that had just come up from headquarters that we referred to as "Memo #2." I can't tell you what Memo #1 was, but #2 sure got our attention. This memo cut our vacation time from sixty to forty-five days. It was primarily driven by the misbehavior and excesses of some Volunteers in one of the groups that had come before ours, turning their time in the country into an extended vacation, abandoning their work sites and traveling too far or too often. Our group had none of that sort of behavior going on, and there was a lot of righteous indignation being evidenced.

Our anger was increased by the fact that Memo #2 also required that fifteen of those forty-five vacation days be taken at Christmas time. So, what had been sixty days to be used as we pleased was now cut down to thirty. Plans that had been made, such as mine, with a swing around South America, needed to be cancelled or severely modified. For example, I had included Brazil in my original tour. Discussions with our Area Reps, calls and/or telegrams to Watson, Baird and other higher ups availed us nothing.

There was a lot of complaining about how the Peace Corps

was turning into just another red-tape filled, top-down driven bureaucracy. The reality was that sixty days was initially established so Volunteers (who were not permitted to go home) would be able to see a great portion of the country they served, rather than just their assigned area. If they chose, they could do some extended travel as well. We were required to stay in the area we served, A, B, or C, unless on vacation or given permission to travel. So, the troops were not happy. And unhappy troops can sometimes do things to put sand in the wheels of progress or act out in ways that are out of character and out of bounds. In my case, I was not angry, but I did find myself out of bounds.

I got up the next day, stiff and tired after sleeping on the floor for about four hours. I read and dozed in the morning. It was nice to be on my mini vacation. We went off to our officially approved Alaskan restaurant that served the American fare. A hot dog can taste pretty good after a steady diet of rice, pork, and bananas for weeks on end. And there was ice cream that was safe to eat! While we were there, Gerry told me they were going to take Wally back to his post and invited me to come along. This was my chance to see the *Oriente*, the side of Ecuador that borders the Amazon region, a place unlike any other part of the country. I had no plans and jumped at the chance.

Early the next day, we loaded up the Jeep with a big battery that was to power Wally's HAM radio, some other items he needed, and off we went. The winding trip up to and then down from the mountains to the east was fantastic. I felt like a V.I.P. on tour, with Wally providing a narrative of the area as if he were reading from a travel brochure. I was awed by huge kapok trees, the baobab trees with trunks that reminded me of a hippopotamus, and other exotic flora and fauna I had never experienced before. My camera got a real workout. (Unfortunately, I loaned my camera to Joe, and somehow all my film got wet, so I have no photos of any value to share from this trip.) About half-way to Zamora, it dawned on me that I was very much out of my assigned work area. Zamora was a much longer trip than I had envisioned. I hadn't asked permission nor had I even told my Area Rep where I was going, Approval would have taken two days to be granted. I had just "gone along for the ride," and if caught or injured while here, I could be in deep trouble. I thought our trip would be a one-day thing, but as it turned out we were to stay the night in Zamora at the home of a Volunteer, George Bennett, whom I had never met. That night I discovered we were not finished with our journey. We were to go even further down country. I figured I should get some details of this trip down in my journal in case it became an issue. And I'm glad I did.

Wally wanted to take a fifty-five-gallon drum of gasoline down river with him, so we removed the back seat of the Jeep to accommodate the drum. After the customary level of Ecuadorian delays and inspections, we got underway at about 10:00. We stopped in a little town called Cumbaratza, where Wally retrieved his mail, and got underway again, winding our way back through some of the most beautiful scenery I had seen to date in all of Ecuador. My camera was again working on overtime.

We went as far as we could by road and then helped Wally roll the drum down to the river, and carried his battery and the rest of his things. As we were doing so, who should appear but George, our previous night's host, along with Tom Trail, the Peace Corps Rep for this Area. I thought I was busted, but he said nothing other than, "Hello." I quickly pointed out that I was here because my crew was on vacation. He still said nothing, but I could almost hear him thinking, "What the hell are you doing here, Redfield?" We said our goodbyes to Wally and promised to meet George and Tom back in Cumbaratza for lunch. I spent the time on the way back sweating bullets and preparing my defense for Tom Trail.

When we met for lunch, it took about five minutes before Tom asked, "Why are you here, Jerry?" I said, "Your honor...." (No, not really.) I explained that since my crew was on vacation, I wasn't really AWOL from my school construction assignment, and given the one chance to see the *Oriente,* I'd grabbed it. Memo #2 had said vacation days had been cut because there were so many National Holidays. This was a good example of taking advantage of one of them. After all, one of the missions of the Peace Corps is to take home a valid description and knowledge of the country to be shared with others, and this was my chance to do just that. The road from La Toma to Loja, I argued, is hardly the whole of Ecuador and with our time cut by the fifteen-day Christmas requirement, we had to grab any opportunity. "And in conclusion...." Then I offered up that I thought we were going on a one-day round trip and I would not have actually been out of my assigned area over night. I only found out as we were traveling that we would not return until this morning, which was bit of a stretch for sure, but Joe and Gerry would confirm it if asked. He said I should have sent a telegram. I explained that doing so would have negated the whole opportunity, as it probably would have taken two days to get the approval.

The three of us got into a big discussion with Tom about the change in leave policy and how we were being punished for the "sins of the fathers," the previous groups who, by the way, had not received any restrictions on their travel. Apparently, it was too late to make any difference. We were pleased to find out that Tom seemed sympathetic to our whining, but sympathy didn't change the facts of the matter. We said our good-byes at about 4:30 and headed out, but not before Trail gave me one more parting shot, reminding me I was off-base, and we would see what John Smith would have to say about it. So, my "trial" had only resulted in kicking my case up to a higher court. Tom would communicate with Smith, and I would have to continue to sweat out the consequences.

Two weeks later, in La Toma, I woke up to a knock on my door and a voice saying, "We want something to eat." I opened the door and there were John Smith and none other than Eugene Baird, the chief of the whole Program in Ecuador! As I was getting ready to go out for breakfast with them, Smith said he had to "mildly reprimand me" for not sending a telegram on the Zamora trip, but that he understood the situation. That made my day and put a nice "period" on the Zamora episode.

We went to breakfast and talked from 8:30 to 11:00 about a lot of subjects: leave policy, the progress on the school here, and my feelings about being here in La Toma. John Smith said that there were a lot of unhappy Volunteers in Loja and among them were Joe Orr and Gerry Mussett. I knew about Gerry, of course, as he was frustrated about everything: the program, the people, the conditions, you name it. Smith said he would be talking with them.

He also said they were discussing starting on another school in a town called Gonzonamá. The town was forty-three miles to the south, up higher up in the mountains, colder, and pretty dead compared to La Toma. I had seen it on my trip with Engineer Ruilloba and wasn't impressed. Eugene Baird summed up by saying I was doing a good job here and I "didn't have to worry about those memos." A good pat on the back was worth a lot at that point and I got it from the top guy! There were no additional vacation days, but certainly a good bit of positive reinforcement. I got the impression that if I could get some other projects going here, I could stay in La Toma. They said they would try and get me the English books I ordered, and John promised me I could get the Cinva-Ram machine I requested from Watson when I needed it. The Zamora episode had come and gone, and I was still in good graces.

DAY BY DAY

WHEN I RETURNED FROM ZAMORA, I HAD GOTTEN INTO A PRETTY regular routine of heading to the school site, working most of the day, and teaching my classes at night. The school consisted of two separate buildings mirroring one another with what would become a playground or assembly area for the students in the middle. They were to be all brick and poured cement structures with large wrought iron windows and would create a more modern and welcoming environment for educating the youth of La Toma. We had been through a couple of *minga* sessions bringing in the town's contribution of sand, rocks and the gravel needed for the foundation. Luckily, in La Toma, this was aided by the contribution of some of the Guarderas trucks and the labor of some of the troops from the army barracks to help in the process. It was a real difference maker compared to what we had to do in Cangonamá. I was helping with the forming and pouring of the columns and the poured beams that would form the frame for the building. The columns and the frames required rebar, and a good amount of labor was involved in putting them together, given the rather primitive state of the construction process. The cement and mortar were still mixed in small batches, bucket brigaded up ladders, and poured into the forms. The bricks were being brought in and laid as soon as they arrived. The place was slowly looking like a building, or two buildings. My role had turned into a combination of supervisor, worker, hod carrier, metal bender, sometime brick layer and whatever else was needed at the direction of *Maestro* Illescas. My other function was to keep track of the material needs: to let the proper people know when things needed to be ordered, when they should be delivered, and if they didn't show up. Additionally, I was to record what had been used and report that up to Justo. From time to time, I also worked in the other direction and became the "union representative" and/or the arbitrator when the workers were not being paid on time or when the brick maker refused a shipment until he was paid.

On one of my trips into Loja to get supplies, I went to the offices of the Loja Public Works Department. I learned that was the place to procure the cement bases for the much-discussed latrine projects. I discovered each one would cost forty sucres. (You may remember we rented our Cangonamá room for sixty sucres per month.) While that was a modest amount in dollars, it was probably a knock out factor for the numbers of latrines we had envisioned. People had already contributed to the school construction fund and to hit them up again would probably not go over very well. It didn't. I informed the people interested in the project, and it seemed to dim their interest, but I hadn't given up yet.

I returned to teaching my classes at night, and this is the point at which I had finally succumbed to the pressure to separate the men from the women. It was a win-win all around. The second class was more mature and included mostly teachers, so I had left that intact. I was still missing the books, but with the help of a teachers' manual, I continued to tap dance my way through the classes until they arrived.

My mid-day and afternoons were still filled with correspondence, reading and paper work. There were a few variations to that routine, depending on who might come calling. One of the people who had come by shortly after John Smith and Baird visited was Justo Andrade. Justo said he had met with Smith and Baird in Catacocha (that bus stop on the way to and from Cangonamá) and they had told him they were pleased with my work here to date. It was nice to hear and good to know that they were not just blowing smoke when they had talked to me after my Zamora episode.

Justo and I went up to talk to the director of the current girls' school and had a good conversation with her. Remember, I had been talked into giving some basketball lessons. I was scheduled to start my basketball training the next week. I had written home to my mother (an English teacher at Pewaukee High) to see if she could get the basketball coach, Bob Thomas (also my American History and Government teacher), to help me by sending charts of some of the plays we had used when he was my coach. I could remember a few but needed more. While we were there, the director also twisted my arm and got me to agree to teach one class of English per week to her sixth-grade class. I agreed to do so, but I'm not sure if it was to impress Justo or just to be accommodating. At least it was one more thing I could do to justify sticking around La Toma.

Occasionally my days would sometimes take me back and forth to Loja either by bus or getting a ride with one of the Guarderas students from my class. On some weekends I would stay in town with Gerry and Joe, and we would catch a movie, read or just hang out. As I had mentioned, it was always a good escape, to not have to be "on," to speak English, and to just kick back with guys with whom I had been through a lot. It was good to have somebody you could complain to who understood because they had been through something similar. We would complain about the customs or habits that we thought were stupid or pick on our most irritating administrative type in the program. A lot of ethnocentric thinking going on no doubt, but it was a good release.

You can imagine my surprise then when I headed into Loja the following weekend and found the apartment almost empty. Gerry left me a note explaining that John Smith had wasted no time making his decision about Gerry's fate. His note said he had been sent up to Cuenca to find out about his new assignment, and Joe was immediately sent out to work with Wally Benson in Zamora. It was a real shock and a pretty lonely feeling to have my two best friends gone, and gone without a word. I went off to see a movie by myself, *Written on the Wind*, starring Lauren Bacall. She reminded me of one of my crushes from church camp so it was a lovely visual escape, and in English!

The next day I ran into Joe Kelly and Armond Joyce and the three of us went to see *The Longest Day*. They informed me that Wally Benson had picked up the lease on the apartment, so it was good to know I would still have a place to crash, even if it would be a pretty lonely place without the other guys. I tried to cheer up the next day watching a soccer game between members of the Guarderas group and a Loja team and then headed back to prepare for a very big event.

Padre Arias, Justo Andrade, Maestro Illescas, and Justo's driver discuss construction progress.

THE AMBASSADOR & AMBASSADORS OF SONG

One of the things the *junta* was big on was to implement the programs under the Alliance for Progress. The many projects under that program only required that the Ecuadorian government contribute twenty per cent of the costs. That was one of the reasons the project's payments were often delayed as they had trouble even coming up with that. Therefore, our school construction projects had some high visibility. This was evidenced by the fact that Maurice Bernbaum, U. S. Ambassador to Ecuador, was coming along with James Watson and other officials to visit our school site and a number of other sites in Loja.

The ambassador and his entourage were due to arrive at 7:00 a.m. at the La Toma airport, and like so many things in Ecuador, the plane was late. All the school kids were lined up along the road in their best outfits to welcome them. We, the locals, waited patiently, and Justo and Engineer Ruilloba arrived around 8:30. The plane finally arrived at 10:00 a.m. As the flags of both countries waved in the breeze, Justo, Ruilloba, and the local bigwigs went out on the runway to welcome Ambassador Bernbaum and Watson with much fanfare. I stayed on the sidelines through twenty minutes of speeches about the importance of the fine work the U. S. was doing for Ecuador, and finally we headed for the school site.

By this time all the kids had marched back into town and were lined up in rows on each side of the entrance to the work site. Padre Arias spoke about the progress and the efforts of the locals and mentioned that there was also a Peace Corps Volunteer working here with them. I was about two feet away from Ambassador Bernbaum when the Padre mentioned it, but he didn't seem interested enough to ask who or where that Volunteer might be, and nobody bothered to tell him that I was right behind him. Maybe later, I thought.

The VIPs all headed over to the local hotel for breakfast, but I didn't go because there just wasn't any room left in the place. Padre Arias came out after they finished and told me to come in and talk to Watson. I asked him about the letter I had sent asking for the Cinva-Ram machine, and he initially said he never received it. Then, in retrospect, he said maybe he just had not found it, because his desk was always full of letters. I found that hard to believe since I had sent it in early February and this was now the 5th of March. A few more speeches ensued, and Justo asked me to go along into Loja. I think he was aware that I hadn't been introduced to the ambassador, and perhaps he thought maybe it could happen there. Since I wanted to meet him, given some long-term aspirations to join the Foreign Service, I jumped at the chance.

We headed for Loja in a big caravan of very official looking cars and a few well-traveled Peace Corps Jeeps. When we got to the entrance of the next stop in Loja, another school, I got out and engaged in conversation with the U. S. Navy pilots that had flown the ambassador down here while he and the others were listening to welcoming speeches and receiving flowers from a group of school girls. Then they all went into the school, and I was left behind. I decided I had about enough of "tagging along." Since there was to be a big reception at the inauguration of that completed school later in the day, I decided to go over to the apartment to clean up and rest.

When I got there, I was surprised to find Gerry, along with Doug, whom I hadn't seen in weeks, and Chuck Jennings who had come down from Cuenca to help Gerry move his stuff up to his new site. I was thrilled to see them all. We shot the breeze for a while, went to lunch, and then headed back to the apartment to engage in the rare custom of putting on suits. We all had brought at least one for special occasions and this was one. We headed over in our "Sunday best" to join in the school inauguration celebration.

Arriving at the school, we found the group already sipping their champagne and getting ready for the big buffet, so nobody paid much attention to our arrival. The official group walked by us on the way to the buffet; the ambassador passed us by; at least Justo offered a brief handshake. Then came our "good friend and fearless leader," James Watson. We noticed he saw us as he came out of the door. He then walked right by all five of us with his head turned as if in intense conversation with someone. We took this as a snub as it appeared a bit too obvious. We couldn't figure out why this was happening, but at this point we decided we had about enough of the big wigs for one day and took off to a local restaurant and had our own celebration. In retrospect, the reality was that in the broad scheme of things, we were the proverbial "pimple(s) on the ass of progress," in this case, the Alliance for Progress. The "higher ups" were there for the long haul, and they saw our group and others like us come and go. However, we thought of ourselves as instrumental, frontline workers and some recognition would have been nice. Watson may have had better relationships with some of the Volunteers in the Quito area, but he sure didn't make much effort down here in Loja.

After our little private celebration, we went back to the

apartment, and changed back into our usual attire. The five of us (Gerry, Doug, Chuck, Jim and I) then headed out to a local park. Doug had arranged for Chuck to serenade a couple young ladies there. Chuck was an excellent guitar player, and he had entertained a lot of us during our training days. He was six-foot plus, with thick, curly blond hair and a winning smile. He stood out among us and certainly stood out among most Ecuadorians who averaged about five feet six inches tall. When kids saw Chuck with his guitar, they all gathered around and soon there were about thirty of them. Chuck sang one song to Doug's friends, and by this time a few more adults showed up as well. Within fifteen minutes there were about 120 people gathered, and they kept us busy singing the folk songs of the era for about an hour. We tried to get away once, but they closed in on us asking for more so we did a few encores. We eventually had worked through our repertoire, and we were tired. Finally, when we tried again to leave, we figured our best ploy would be to walk away singing. Well, they just followed along for about seven blocks until we reached the apartment. We were the Pied Pipers of Loja. We played one last song outside and made a break for the door. Once we were safely inside, the crowd stood down below shouting and hollering for more. Chuck, Gerry and I, the best singers in the group, went to the window and sang three more and then finally closed up.

The next thing we heard was a loud clamber on the stairs as part of the group came up the stairs shouting and pounding on the door for more. We didn't give them any more so they turned out our lights from the breaker box down below. We sat quietly in the dark for about a half hour, and the group finally gave up and dwindled away. We couldn't believe the positive impact we had, as the songs we sang were all American folk songs like "Blowin' in the Wind," "Tom Dooley," "Walk Right In," "Michael Row the Boat Ashore," and other popular songs of the day. I thought we made a very good trio and was again disappointed that Chuck and Gerry would be heading off to Cuenca. We capped the evening off at another Volunteer's place eating American style fresh corn on the cob. It was the "frosting on the cake" of one of the most memorable evenings I had in the country during my service.

ONE LAST HURRAH!

I WOKE UP THE NEXT DAY IN LOJA FEELING BAD ABOUT GERRY and Chuck heading out the next day for Cuenca. As fortune would have it, I did have a chance to see them there one more time. I had a cracked filling that could only be handled by the Peace Corps approved dentist in Cuenca. I made reservations on a decent bus line from Loja to Cuenca for the next day thinking I might catch up with Gerry and Chuck while in Cuenca to visit the dentist. But, to honor my commitment to teaching, I returned to La Toma, with the intention of going back to Loja on the 8:30 bus that evening. I conducted my first two classes, but missed the bus back into Loja, so I taught the third class as well. I waited in my room, thinking I might catch a *mixto* coming through that night. (None did.) While I was waiting, Marlene, her sister Yolanda, Luis, Carlos and his brother Wilson came up to my room. The group crowded in with a record player and an English language record. They played the record, talked and stayed until 11:30.

To catch my 9:00 a.m. bus from Loja to Cuenca, I got up at 5:30 the next day feeling pretty groggy, and caught a *mixto* heading to Loja at 6:15. That morning marked eight months in the program, and it was starting to feel like I had spent most of it on, or waiting for, busses, Jeeps, trucks and *mixtos* from La Toma to Loja and back.

When I got into Loja, I discovered that Gerry and Chuck had not yet left. Joe Orr had come in from Zamora, and they decided to stay another day to spend some time with him. We all went to breakfast together before I successfully caught my bus to Cuenca. I arrived at about 4:00 and met with Ed Delci, with whom I was staying. Gerry and Chuck showed up later, and we all went out to dinner at one of the many good restaurants that Cuenca offered. Chuck had to leave early to make his regular appearance on a local radio station. He had parlayed his singing prowess into a radio gig, and it was going over very well. We enjoyed listening to it as we ate. This was another example of good PR in Cuenca, and I just wished we had as good an opportunity in Loja, where PR clearly was at a minimum. When Chuck returned, we headed out to a birthday party for the Ecuadorian wife of one of the Volunteers from an earlier program. It was so nice to have a *trago* free, quiet social occasion with no dour looking chaperones, no bright lights, and with familiar American records on the phonograph – a welcome touch of home.

The next day was a Sunday, and we spent it just hanging out. We joined up with Volunteer Noble Wiltshire and took him out to the seminary where he was doing some work. The local padres invited us in to watch a play they were presenting. Gerry, Chuck and I deferred, but Noble felt obligated and stayed. We picked him up later, played a little basketball and went to the Hotel Cuenca, the home of that excellent and inexpensive steak dinner that I had enjoyed earlier. I repeated the experience.

On Monday I got my authorization for the dentist from Doc Caplin and had the cracked filling replaced. While the dentist was prowling around in my mouth he discovered four small cavities, so I returned in the afternoon to have those fixed. In the interim, I went to the Peace Corps Office and picked up the English books that had finally arrived. What were shipped were only twenty books (all they had, they said), and they were only the Part I editions of what we had ordered. Smith had promised both sets at the price my students had paid! My students were expecting a complete set for their thirty sucres, and I was not looking forward to showing them these books. In addition to getting the English books, I was excited to see they had also sent the other books I had requested: Community Development, Adobe Construction, Latrine Building, and How to Form Co-operatives. The last one, along with some other Alliance "propaganda," was something that I hoped to use with Suco and the Centro Cultural.

Chuck came over to Ed's and said that Noble wanted us for dinner at his place, so we went. Ed cooked up tortillas and apple pie which was supplemented with a case of fine Ecuadorian Pilsner beer. Noble and I got into an impromptu Smother's Brothers act, then out came Chuck's guitar, and we sang far into the night. It was a memorable "wrap" to my last hurrah with these guys for a long, long while. It was time to get back to work in La Toma.

A GUY NAMED "JOSÉ"

I ARRIVED IN LA TOMA THE NEXT DAY, ALL FIRED UP AND READY to spread the bad news about the books and share my newfound knowledge of latrine building, co-ops and more. I had come from Loja on a 7:00 a.m. bus and went right to the worksite only to discover that the cement we ordered had not come in. In addition, we were running low, and the boards that were to build the forms for the topmost cement beam had also not arrived as ordered nor had the rebar. There was another trip back to Loja in the stars. I then went over to talk to Padre Arias about the latrine information I had gathered, but his ardor for latrine building had apparently faded. He was now more interested in getting light poles and lamps installed. If the good Padre wasn't interested, the odds were that my envisioned plan of latrines for the masses was going to die aborning.

That evening I managed to pass out the English books to the classes without too much trouble, but a few folks, as I suspected they would, felt they'd been had. However, the books gave some much needed structure to the classes. Things went relatively well from that point on.

I checked in with Suco and shared the information from the Alliance for Progress material I had picked up, and he then knocked my socks off by asking if I had anything on co-operatives. Whoo boy! Do I have anything on co-operatives? You bethcha!

I took the information I had to him, and he said he wanted to use it later. I wondered if this might be more talk or if it could be the start of something good. I needed to have one of these projects "click" if I was to be allowed to stay here when the school was completed. I decided to get a letter off to a Volunteer who specialized in co-op development to see what he had, and to find out if he would be willing to talk with Suco and the other members of the Cultural Center if they were interested. I didn't know enough about the mechanics of starting a co-op to be of help.

I was really beginning to get downhearted. I was getting nowhere with my ideas to date, so I delved into the book on Community Development. It strongly suggested working through civic organizations and clubs that already existed. There were a number in La Toma, and since not much had come of my initial attempts, I thought I would check out some of them to see what their reaction would be. However, the "biggest dog in the pack" was the *Centro Cultural,* the Cultural Center of which Suco was the heavy hitter, and they had a tendency to look down upon other groups. That was my impression, and I decided I should proceed with caution.

I went to Marlene's home to see if she could give me some pointers or advice on how to work with some of the "players" in town and identify some of the groups that I could approach. Her mother ran a small fabrics and notions store, and that's where we talked, out in front of the store on a couple of chairs. (Wouldn't want people to talk but, of course, they did.) Through Carlos and the Carrión family, she had become a good friend and acquaintance, as well as a frequent dance partner at those many dances that accompanied every holiday. She was smart, confident and bold enough to speak her mind. In addition to discussing the information I wanted about the groups, we talked about why I thought some of their social customs (the multiple holidays; the *trago;* the need to separate the sexes, even at mature ages; the requirements for chaperones at every turn) were just out of a different era. In retrospect, what was going on was probably not unlike what happened in the U. S. in the roaring 1920's. There were *some* willing to see things change, but the Catholic Church and the older generation were holding firm, while the younger folk were ready for change.

Marlene heard me out, but her view was that, in her experience, so many of the men of La Toma were *brutos*: crude, vulgar types with only one thing on their mind. And her mother, I suspect, thought the same thing. I hoped I could change both their minds. However, I <u>had</u> been in the country for five months.... As time went on, sitting on that front porch, I found her and her advice, opinions, and company of great value and comfort.

The bulk of these March days were filled by alternating between trips to the school, coaching the girls' basketball teams, and preparing for my English classes. I spent much of my free time taking care of my correspondence: with Ann, who was still dutifully writing every day; to my parents; a couple of ex-girlfriends, Sally Meyer and Nadine Nass; college pals, including Chip Lee, John Skornika and John Haggstrom; a few other Peace Corps Volunteers, including my high school classmate, Greg Schaefer, who was serving in Columbia; and friends from my hometown.

The evening classes were going fairly well. I had just finished up with the first two classes one night and was about to start the 8:00 class when there was such a commotion outside our classroom door that I couldn't possibly go on. I opened the door and there were fireworks going off. A "wild bull" was running through the crowd chasing people who ran screaming and trying to get out of its way. This bull was actually a man wearing a large paper mâché bull's head with horns that shot out sparks. It was the eve of San José (Saint Joseph) Saint's Day, and since the town was filled with people named José, they were really going to do it up right.

Saint Joseph's Day arrived, and what a day it was! I went over to the school worksite at about 8:30 and found two very hungover workers and some other people who were eager to play volley ball. None of the other usually reliable workers (one named José) were on the scene either. The man who runs the warehouse for the project was also named José, and it did not take long to figure that the whole crew had spent most of the night and into the morning celebrating their Saint's Day at José's house. At about 9:00, the rest of the crew came stumbling out of the house. I said, "I understand the situation. Don't worry. We'll just add a couple hours of overtime to make up for what you missed." They looked at me with bleary eyes and ambled over to pick up some boards which they promptly used to prop themselves up. I asked them if they would like to make it <u>three</u> hours of overtime to make up the work. They shook their heads, decided they just didn't have it in them to continue, and we should just count this day as lost.

There was a big party brewing for "our" José. *Maestro* Illescas invited me in for a beer, sheepishly fawned over me and profusely apologized for not being in any condition to work. He was clearly worried that I would hold it against him. I told him that I understood, not to worry about it, and that all I cared about was that we properly entered the day as "taken off" in the record books - and it was.

You might be getting the impression that I was accustomed to drinking in the morning. That wasn't the case, but the degree to which *trago* was consumed on every occasion and every business transaction was amazing. This morning's imbibing for them was just a continuation of the previous evening's adventure but not for me. I took my exit as soon as I had tipped a couple of shots to salute the "honoree." With more maturity and the wisdom that comes with age, I would have worried much less about offending anyone and told them I had a medical condition that prevented me from drinking the stuff. However, as a twenty-two-year-old "kid," sensitive to being accepted and not wanting to offend, I had already lost the ability to pull that ploy. I had become in many people's minds "one of the guys" which was a goal, but the manner by which I was meeting that goal meant I was paying for it at the danger of ruining my health and my liver.

WHEN YOU CARE ENOUGH

As I headed back to my room, I ran into Jim Snyder who had come out with a group of workers to deal with the town's septic system. Jim was a civil engineer, and though he trained with our group, his skill set was best used in dealing with water systems so he ended up working with the Loja Municipality that served the area. We had lunch, and then I joined him and his workers to learn more about it. I took a break in the afternoon to go coach the girls' basketball team only to discover nobody had the keys to the room where the basketball was kept, so back I went to finish up with Jim and his crew.

Jim joined me for dinner, and surprised me with a letter he was delivering. It was quite a surprise indeed. My small-town Pewaukee High School had raised money and sent me a $64.00 (worth about $600 in today's value) CARE donation. The La Toma teachers were often complaining that there was just no money for supplies, etc., etc., and nobody seemed to want to contribute any more. This donation was a godsend. It was supposed to include a list from which to choose things, but it wasn't attached. Fortunately, I had a brochure that I received in training, entitled *How to Help Peace Corps Volunteers Through CARE*. With that donation I was able to order two physical education kits that totaled four dodge balls, two soccer balls, two volley balls and nets, an inflator and two basketballs. I also ordered a needle trades kit, which the local home economics sewing group needed badly. It included several types of scissors, darning needles, crochet hooks, and a variety of thread, needles and other notions related to sewing. And the $64.00 donation wasn't depleted yet. I still had seven dollars left, and with that I added an elementary student kit that could be used in the recreation center and a "Village Library" that included materials for literacy courses and a number of booklets on things like child care, pure water and hygiene. Not exactly a library, but it was a start. All I could say and did when I wrote to thank them was, "God bless PHS!" This was how the Peace Corps was supposed to be making things happen by making it a nationwide effort, not just another bureaucracy about which most people knew little.

The Peace Corps got a lot of publicity back home at the time. It was a unique and different approach to foreign affairs. From my small hometown of about 2,000 people, there were no less than six or seven from my high school serving in seven different countries. (A lot of the credit goes to the faculty, in my opinion.) Parents of the Volunteers were known to keep in touch with each other, so their awareness of those countries was certainly much higher than it would have been without the Corps. They were eager to do what they could to support our efforts. As evidence of that support, two basketball playbooks from my former coaches, Bob Thomas and Ron Feuerstein, arrived in the mail. Watch out for my girls now!

As it turned out, the arrival of the playbooks was well timed, for the Centro Cultural was sponsoring a big sports festival and a dance. There were basketball and soccer matches planned, as well as car races, and number of other competitive events. I hoped to have my teams ready for their participation. I coached them from 4:30 to 6:00 every night of the following week. Supposedly I had two teams, one from the school's sewing club and the other from the homemaking group, but since three-fourths of the players were in both groups, it was pretty much an intramural contest. On the day of the games, however, they would be flying different flags.

LOSING FAITH?

THE LAST FEW WEEKS OF MARCH HAD BEEN A REAL BATTLE. THE back-and-forth trips to Loja, the crazy interruptions in the classes and the work site, and the inability to close the deal on some of the projects were getting me down. I would go into Loja and try to lighten up by going to a movie or two on the weekends, but the delays in delivery of materials, the efforts to find Mario Mena and get no satisfaction were getting to be a drag. I had developed another very bad cold and an almost constant hack and decided this might be a good time to quit smoking again. And, no doubt, the many persuasive invitations to go out for "a drink" were not helping either. I could choose to stay in my windowless room with its sixty-watt bulb flickering away, and many nights I did. However, my closest Volunteer friends had shipped out for other parts, so I did welcome the companionship that those invites provided.

My background included a fairly solid religious training and practice. I was raised within the Methodist faith, had done my share of Bible study, and for a time considered entering the ministry. I'd even endured the tugs and challenges to faith that come with the college scene. I came out as a believing and open-minded Protestant if not a regular church going adult since graduation. I had gone with Gerry to Mass at Christmas in Quito and in Loja. I even bought a missal before coming to La Toma thinking that perhaps I would be going to services there, but to this point I hadn't. The practices and services I had attended were still being delivered in Latin, with lots of incense, and sometimes a weird mix of Catholic and indigenous customs were employed. Even the Catholic Volunteers couldn't figure what was going on half the time, given the mix of Catholic and indigenous rituals and practices during Mass.

The reality was that I hadn't darkened the door of the good Padre's church since I had been in La Toma. My absence may have been noted by him, perhaps, but since I usually spent so many of my weekends in Loja, I don't think it was an issue with most people. Generally, it was the women, both young and old, and older men who attended. But Easter week was here, and like churches everywhere, Easter brings in even the slackers. However, there was one glaring exception – me.

Thursday night I went over to eat at Suco's at about 6:00. There were only a few others there, and I noticed that nobody was eating. I thought maybe everyone else was abstaining or they were at Mass. I remembered my Episcopal friends back home never ate before taking communion and thought maybe that was it. Maundy Thursday had never been a big thing in my practice, so I wasn't too familiar with what was going on. It's the commemoration of the "Last Supper," but in my memory I can't remember attending a service at home. I went in and had a couple of Cokes with two of the Guarderas workers, and I ordered dinner. While we were talking, Suco closed the doors, saying that some people complained if he stayed open during Mass. He brought me my dinner, and I dined by myself. I asked him if I was screwing up, doing something wrong by eating. He said, "No." But I felt like I was the only person in town eating that night. After people got out of Mass, and as I left Suco's, I overheard them talk about how wonderful and meaningful the service was to them. I felt really out of it.

On Good Friday morning, it appeared that everybody was heading to the church again for Mass or confession. I didn't know which. So, I went over Suco's to see if anybody was eating breakfast and nobody was. I stood around for a while, and when nobody else came, I bought a couple of rolls from a little kiosk outside the restaurant and had breakfast in my room. I wanted to make sure I wasn't going to make the same mistake I had made the night before. Maybe they were fasting all week until Sunday? When I went to Suco's place later on he asked me why I hadn't come in for breakfast. I gave him some excuse about how I decided not to eat that morning and that seemed to fit in well because he asked me if I was fasting. I mumbled something and quickly changed the subject. I was thinking to myself, "Being a Protestant around here during Holy Week is like being a gentile at the Fontainebleau Hotel in Miami during tourist season."

I went back to my room, and at about 10:00 a.m., Doc Caplin, Joe Orr, Wally Benson, Jim Snyder, and Doug Strauss showed up. They said they were on their way to Cariamanga and asked if I wanted to go along. I jumped at the chance. The dilemma of "to go or not to go to Mass" was solved. Cariamanga, a town about forty-five miles to the south, was notorious for selling contraband items from Peru, and one could always find something of interest there. Away we all went, shopped, caught up with one of the Volunteers now serving there, returned to get my things and went to Loja for the Easter weekend. I saw *The Bridges at Toko-Ri* and we played some baseball. I didn't go to church and I felt like a real slacker.

Doc Caplin stretches his legs as we wait (again) for Caterpillars to clear a path on the Pan-Am Highway.

...AND WHILE I WAS OUT

January, February and March, 1964

Politics:

- Republican Barry Goldwater declares his candidacy for president.
- Margaret Chase Smith, the first female senator from Maine, declares her candidacy for the Republican nomination for president and becomes the first woman to be placed in nomination at the convention of a major political party.
- The Supreme Court rules that congressional districts must be approximately the same size.
- The Supreme Court declares that under the First Amendment, speech criticizing political figures cannot be censored.

Civil Rights:

- President Johnson declares War on Poverty.
- The 24th Amendment to the U. S. Constitution is ratified, preventing the use of poll taxes in national elections.
- A Jackson, Mississippi, jury decides it cannot reach a verdict in the trial of Byron De La Beckwith for the murder of Medgar Evers.
- The House of Representatives passes the Civil Rights Act sent by JFK in June of 1963.

- Cassius Clay meets with Malcom X and others and announces the next morning that he has converted to the anti-integrationist Nation of Islam.
- Malcom X is suspended from The Nation of Islam, resigns and announces he is forming the Black Nationalist Party.

Vietnam:

- Routine patrols by the U. S. Navy begin in the South China Sea.
- President Johnson rejects President de Gaulle's offer of a peace settlement for Vietnam.
- General Nguyen Khanh overthrows the President of Vietnam in a coup.
- In Saigon, Army of the Republic of Vietnam (ARVN) forces surround the Viet Cong but allow them to slip away.
- U. S. Defense Secretary McNamara reiterates U. S. intention to provide increased military and economic aid to Vietnam.

Space:

- Ranger 6 is launched by NASA, carrying television cameras that will be used when it lands on the moon.

International:

- U. S. troops and Panamanian civilians clash in the Panama Canal Zone resulting in the deaths of twenty-one Panamanians and four U. S. soldiers.
- Cuba cuts off the water supply to the U. S. base at Guantanamo Bay Naval Base in retaliation for seizure of Cuban fishing boats off of Florida.
- The Brazilian military, backed by the U. S., overthrows President Joao Goulart in a bloodless coup, initiating twenty-one years of dictatorship.

- The Arab League, a confederation of fourteen Arab states creates the Palestine Liberation Organization (PLO), designates Israel as an illegal state, and vows to eliminate Zionism from Palestine.

Culture:

- The Beatles arrive at JFK International Airport greeted by 25,000 screaming fans and "Beatlemania" is born in the U. S.
- The Beatles appear on the Ed Sullivan Show and are viewed by 73 million people. Their arrival forms the catalyst for the "British Invasion" that followed, including The Rolling Stones, The Who, Dave Clark Five, Herman's Hermits and others.
- The first statement from the U. S. Surgeon General declares that "smoking may be hazardous to one's health."
- Cassius Clay defeats Sonny Liston in Miami, becoming the Heavy Weight Champion of the World, and meets with Malcolm X, Sam Cooke, and Jim Brown afterwards. (A fictional account of the evening became a play and later an award-winning film, *One Night in Miami.*)
- The first Ford Mustang comes off the assembly line at Ford Motors, selling over 100,000 cars between April and July. Other low cost "sporty" cars would soon flood the U. S. market.

CENTERING ON THE CENTRO CULTURAL

When I arrived in La Toma from my get away Easter weekend, I checked to see if the *maestro* and his crew had returned safely. They had. I was trying to fight off the cold that had become much worse. It was probably the same one that had been hanging around since the beginning of Lent. It had been dragging me down for the last month, and all the invitations to go out over the last month hadn't helped one bit.

I decided to take the day off and talk to Padre Arias. He told me that they used to have a 4-H Club in La Toma about six years prior. After meeting with the Padre, I met with Suco while I had lunch. His opinion was that the club hadn't been much of a success. Apparently, some disease had hit the livestock. A veterinarian couldn't get out from Loja in time, and all the animals died. However, he said that if we did start another club, we could meet in the facilities of the Centro Cultural. Since my experience with the 4-H was limited to the bird house I had tried to build, I figured I had better call in some help on this one.

Suco and I also talked a little about the plans for the upcoming week, and he teased me about my girls' basketball teams in a good-natured way. Then we got into discussing what was needed for the community. He pulled out a big book with the by-laws for the Centro Cultural group and showed me all the letters they had written to try to get support. He also told me about some of the projects they were currently doing around the community, and I formed a better opinion of the club. Apparently, if things were to happen it would be through them. As I mentioned, this organization was the "biggest dog in the pack." I figured, with the right amount of politicking, that's where I would have to center my effort. However, what Suco reminded me of was important as well. For the moment, he said, the important thing was to complete the school construction. "True," I thought, "but if I don't have something in the pipeline to show Smith and company for a reason to stay, I'll be shipped off to Gonzanamá *or who knows where!"*

The Cultural Center's 19th Anniversary Celebration came off on the following weekend but with the usual delays. This was one of the few times I became a "tourist" and pulled out my hand cranked movie camera and filmed some of the activities, including "The (Not So) Great Race." I went up to the top of a nearby hill that was high enough to capture the whole valley: the lush green growth down the road, as well as the dust bowl in which we lived. I took in the airport to the west of town and the strange collection of cars and trucks (an early fifties Buick convertible, pick-up trucks, jeeps, panel trucks, a Range Rover, and even a couple of Guarderas gravel trucks) gunning their engines and kicking up dust in the plaza.

In the process I captured some footage of a Saraguro "Indian" (as we called them at the time before political correctness) who had come for the festivities. The Saraguros are the descendants of the Incas (now spelled "Inka" in a PC effort to reassert the pronunciation of the original Quechua language) who once ruled all of the Andes. The women wear black ponchos fastened by decorative, long-stemmed pins and wear large traditional straw hats or black fedoras. The men wear black pants the length of pedal pushers or capris and also wear fedoras but with larger brims and crowns. It is said that their choice of black is meant as mourning for the murder of Inca Chief Atahualpa by the Spanish in 1533. They tend to live in the Andes on their own land and are one of the few tribes who maintained control over their own destiny. There was a large settlement in the Province of Loja, and they would often come to display their wares at city festivals but were seldom seen in La Toma. I was glad to include him in my film.

I went up to the top of another hill to catch the cars and trucks racing from down the valley into town and then dashed to the finish line to catch the winner as he took the flag. I filmed the horse race (of only two horses) and got some footage of one of my girls' basketball teams, unfortunately performing miserably. They seemed to have forgotten everything I had tried to teach them. I ended my role as tourist and joined as a member of the Cultural Centro's basketball team playing against one from Loja. We lost by one point. I hadn't run that much in five years.

For the first time in my four months here in La Toma, I was invited to dine with the Carriõn family for lunch, and I felt good about that. I don't know if it was because I was becoming more accepted or if people thought we "ate differently," but I was glad for the opportunity. Rain wiped out the scheduled soccer games, and I was relieved, for it gave me time to rest up from my basketball effort and get ready for the big *baile*, the dance. It was supposed to start at 8:30, but like everything else that day and in fine Ecuadorian fashion, it started about an hour and a half late. After another hour of ceremonies and speeches commemorating the 19th Anniversary of the Centro, the dancing finally got underway. They made up for the late start by going until 3:00 a.m., amply fueled by great quantities of *trago*.

ON THE BEAM

I PLANNED TO GO INTO LOJA THE NEXT DAY, APRIL 25TH, TO CHECK on the delay in materials and line up a truck for hauling them, but no bus arrived, so I headed to work. That day marked six months in Ecuador. The following day I successfully headed back into Loja on the 8:00 a.m. bus to do what it seemed I had spent most of my time doing since starting on this project - hunting down Mario Mena. I filled the rest of the morning trying to find him in order to reserve a truck to haul the rocks and cement we would need to pour the topmost beam that ran the full length and width of the building. I finally found him and the local engineer on their lunch break. At 2:00 I went over to the Municipal yard and got a big supply of wires and nails for the rebar and construction of the forms. I caught a 4:00 bus back that, for some reason, took two hours to get back to La Toma. I arrived just in time to shave, grab a bite and get to class. All that time and effort spent to reserve a truck, deliver a message and get a bucket of nails!

The next night I informed the students that there would be no class on Thursday as we would be pouring the beam then, and it would take all day to get it done. I also told them we would need all the help we could get. We lined up ten helpers and four buckets, but we needed more. I encouraged them to ask their students to bring whatever they could to help. It was *minga* time again.

Thursday was a rainy day and the day to pour the beam. I went over to the site at about 8:30 where I found the crew had already been finalizing the forms and making final placement of the rebar. At about 9:00 we started hand-mixing the cement in large tubs and pouring it, using the four five-gallon buckets we had on hand. I had a surprise visit at about 10:00 from John Smith, Eugene Baird, Doc Caplin and Buster Lewis, the Peace Corps' Director for all of the West Coast Latin American Operations. Wow! Such high visibility. Doc Caplin gave me some much-needed cold pills (I had been operating on six over-the-counter penicillin pills bought at the corner kiosk.) He also informed me that they had dropped off a five-gallon water jug for use at the house and my very own book locker (similar to a footlocker but bigger). They made a few encouraging remarks and were on their way to another site.

Doug Strauss, still doing some work in Buena Vista, stopped by at lunch time on his way to Loja for some vaccinations. We all had to head there on the weekend to get shots for the bubonic plague and a few other nasty tropical diseases. He said the Doc had told him I should be looking for a large thermos of serum that was due in on a plane the next day.

After he left, I checked on my new jug and locker. The book locker wasn't new and contained a hand-me-down set of books from one of the Volunteers who had left the Loja area. However, I was more than glad to get it. Reading was one of the great escapes in this existence and one of my favorite pastimes - and it still is. I was glad to have my own in-house supply. In these earliest days of the Peace Corps, each Volunteer (or Volunteer couple) was given a locker containing about 250 books. The book locker was a Peace Corps perk, full of what the government thought were significant or representative paperback books like Profiles in Courage, The Rise and Fall of the Third Reich, The Tin Drum, Travels with Charley, and over a hundred others as well as a number of informational brochures on building things, such as how to build fly-proof coolers and other handy hints on irrigation, gardening, etc. They were to be read by the Volunteer at his or her leisure and then passed on to another Volunteer or contributed to the local library. The contents changed from year to year. Former Volunteer Jack Priebus wrote about his responsibility of assembling the lockers and notes that the idea for the book lockers came from Eunice Kennedy Shriver, John Kennedy's sister and wife of the Peace Corps Director, Sargent Shriver. As I was rummaging through the books, Volunteers John Mulligan and Bill Fuzetti stopped in to say hello. What a day for visitors! I facetiously invited them to pitch in with the *minga* at the school but didn't find any takers.

I returned to the worksite and discovered that our water supply had run out. I don't know if we had drained the water supply or whether there were other problems, but we had to act fast to keep things going. I went down to the school and, with the teachers' approval, recruited a group of about forty kids to help. They formed a bucket brigade to pass water from a nearby pond full of stagnant but usable water that was then poured into the big tank we used to mix the cement. During the middle of our bucket brigade, it started raining like mad. We were in the ironic position of getting soaked because there was no water!

We kept at it through intermittent showers and ate dinner in shifts. We ran out of cement around 7:30 that night. I ran over to the local purveyor and asked for ten more bags. Even though I didn't have the customary official order from the agency, I convinced him that we were in a crisis situation and he cooperated. It started to rain even harder at this point, and I got one of the Guarderas truck drivers to get a truck and transport the bags over to the school. We kept at it, and at about 9:30 Padre Arias brought over some *trago* and hot water (because "some like it hot") that was passed around. That perked up some people and wiped-out others. Finally, five of my English students showed up to help, and we finished at 11:00 p.m. on the dot. It was a fine example of community in action.

When I got up the next day, my cold was even worse after having been out in the rain all day. It was National Teachers' Day, another day off, and the teachers invited me to a luncheon which I was sure was going to be another *trago* fest. I was saved from all that by the arrival of Smith and company who were on their way back into Loja. Doc Caplin checked my chest again, didn't like what he heard and gave me some cough syrup. I told him that the serum he sent on the plane had not come in here, so it had most likely gone into Loja. They proceeded to do the same - went into Loja. I then gave myself a well-deserved day off. At about 5:00 Padre Arias sent someone over to get me, as the teachers were "still at it," and wanted me to join them for dinner. I figured it was safe because I would be able to excuse myself to teach class. However, after dinner no one could give me a key so classes were cancelled.

A TORTOISE RACE TO THE FINISH

THE MAIN BEAM NOW UP, THE SCHOOL WAS STARTING TO LOOK like a building. What was left was to organize more *mingas* for the gathering of additional rocks, sand and gravel to fill in the floors; the gathering of wood for the roof beams; tile and brick work; and then a repeat of the process for the second wing of the school. Multiply by a factor of five the number of trips into Loja, the hours of waiting for Mario Mena, the late delivery or lack of materials, the failure to pay, and you get some idea of my daily life and times over the next couple of months. The weeks of work on the school were starting to seem like the movie *Ground Hog's Day*, where the main character keeps living the same day over and over. Administrative screw-ups, including late payments or no payments for work and materials; my personally hauling of materials out to La Toma that should have been delivered; and frustrating delays were part of my daily routine. Slowly but surely, the site was turning into a school building, but the progress was agonizingly slow for someone used to big trucks delivering lumber, cranes lifting materials, cement trucks rolling up and pouring out their contents, and work crews using power tools to put it all together.

In the meantime, my "other duties as required," as job descriptions say, my daily efforts to develop some meaningful Community Development projects went on in earnest. I kept hoping that one of them would click, so I could justify staying in La Toma, but as long as the school wasn't finished, no one seemed interested in doing anything else.

One thing that seemed to be working well was my coaching commitment with the girls' school. I thought that after the big Centro Cultural weekend things would die down, but I discovered that May 24th was a big anniversary of another sports club in town, and we had to prepare for that. One of the regular frustrations with this gang was that the ball they use for practice was kept under lock and key, and too often the keeper of the key wasn't around. I couldn't wait for my CARE package to be delivered.

Most of my weekends were spent in Loja, where we would catch the "latest" movie offerings and play a little pick-up basketball. Basketball was a big sport here. Because some people had seen us Volunteers playing in Loja, we received invitations from three schools for our team to play against them. What they didn't know was that our "team" never played a game as a team, but that wasn't about to stop us from trying. I went so far as to ask my mother to send me my Converse basketball shoes, hoping they would "up my game."

I went into Loja for our first game appearance on a Wednesday night. We were supposed to begin the game at 8:00, but it started to rain at about 5:00. After dinner it stopped so it was "game on!" We went over to play at 8:00, but it poured for the next four hours. Our big debut was a washout. It was rescheduled for that Friday night. I was torn between my devotion towards my English classes and "defending the honor of the USA." I hadn't held a class all that week (and it looked like rain again), but all the guys were begging me to stay in Loja so I consented. First there was an indoor soccer game and no rain, then a JV basketball game and no rain. Finally, it was our turn. "*Los Meesteres*" ran out, dressed in our gym shorts, blue tie-dyed T-shirts (I forgot who did it for us) and ridiculous looking straw hats, and we went through our warm-up drills. The game started and we played all of five minutes before the skies opened up again. At that point we were up five to three points, so it wasn't too bad. The sponsors were happy because their efforts had brought in a large crowd, and they were in the chips. We were invited to play a game again the next weekend but it too was rained out.

The Cinva-Ram machine I had ordered finally arrived, and I hoped that it might be useful in a big project. The Chief of Police told me that "when he got his Jeep fixed" we could go down to a nearby *barrio* where they were considering building some latrines for their school. I made up a few blocks for display purposes, thinking that if anybody, anywhere, ever decided to do a latrine project (as they had in other towns) they would see how good the blocks were. One day, a small group from the *barrio* came to look at the blocks but decided it would be too expensive to use, as you have to have mortar to use them. With adobe you just slap mud between them and you've got yourself a wall. I took the machine out to the military barracks, and they experimented with making bricks for the future but couldn't think of any immediate use for them. So, I had a very nice new piece of equipment ready for something, but nothing I could justify to Smith or Justo.

As for the 4-H effort, I had picked up some literature over the weeks and went to talk to Padre Arias about it. He decided that we had to identify a designated leader for the club and get it organized before presenting it to the public. He suggested someone as a leader who I didn't think was a good fit, but it wasn't my call. I sought some information from back home and explored the possibility of a person-to-person, "sister club" possibility, and if anyone knew of an interested party. I talked with members of the Heifer Project in Loja about how they might be of assistance. Around the end of April, I met some of the members from the club that had been formed earlier, and they said that they would be willing to help in the reorganization. It seemed promising, but I wasn't holding my breath. By the middle of May I made three more attempts with the Padre, and he finally said, "Let's wait on that until the school is finished." That seemed to be the order of the day and the same party line I had heard from Suco. I considered the 4-H project a dead issue.

At this time even my English classes weren't going very smoothly. One night, the School Committee called me out of the second class for a meeting to decide about the sewers for the school and what kind of wall they wanted to build around it. A wall! I hated the idea of putting a wall around the place and making it look like a prison. But with the pigs, goats, donkeys, mules and chickens wandering around on the loose, I guessed I would have to bow to the local custom. Not surprisingly, they reached no conclusion and the evening ended. On a subsequent evening, my first class went well, but as I started the second class, the lights went out. Instead of letting me call the class off, three students ran out, got candles and we had class by candlelight. How's that for dedication! The third class, seeing no lights, didn't stick around, so at least I got a little break. Friday of that same week there was no class as it was Ecuador's Labor Day Celebration. My students had informed me that Saturday the 30th would be a big fiesta down the road from La Toma and that I had better be around for it. John Mulligan, who worked for the Municipality of Loja, came through town one day that week and informed me that we had a basketball game scheduled for that Saturday against the University team. It appeared that if I wanted to keep my students happy, I would have a dilemma on my hands that Saturday.

The other piece of bad news I heard during this period was that Gerry had had it with the Peace Corps and was heading home or had already headed home. He had always had issues with John Smith, and apparently their proximity in Cuenca did not help things. We had been pretty close, having had the apartment together, so I was sad to hear that news. Two things of a positive nature kept me from also throwing in the towel at this point. One was the arrival of the items from the CARE package I ordered with all the sports equipment and an interesting, out of the ordinary, request from Smith himself.

On one of my many trips into Loja for materials, I ran into Smith and a Peace Corps evaluator from Washington. They said they would be out to see me the next day. When they arrived, the evaluator, who also wrote articles for *Life, The Saturday Evening Post* and other magazines, asked me a lot of questions about the program. John left me a set of instructions for writing up a case report that might be put into a training manual. I don't know if it was included in the manual, but after reading it 55 years later, I can well understand if it was not used. (See Appendix.) Smith also told me that the August issue of *The Volunteer* (a monthly journal about the Peace Corps written for the Volunteers but also read by parents and others) would be featuring Ecuador so there might be a possibility that my comments from his interview would be in it. (They weren't.)

The other bit of "good news" was that Smith told me that it was okay for me to take my much-anticipated vacation in August. All that remained was to do the paperwork. I could finally give Ann some definitive news. The plan was for Joe Orr, his girlfriend, Ann and me to make the loop around Latin America within the thirty-day window that was left to us since the arrival of the infamous Memo #2. Pat Yoshida, Joe's girlfriend, a Volunteer in the Health Program in Columbia, had trained and become friends with Ann in Albuquerque. At last, there was something of a positive nature to anticipate.

On the down side, I was now having to contemplate the real possibility, the probability of leaving my friends in La Toma, and for all my frustrations with them at times, I had truly fallen in love with the place and the people. The prospect of leaving had me down. The lyrics of "The Exodus Song," would run through my mind as I stood on the balcony of the house overlooking the town and valley below, *"This land is mine, God gave this land to me..."*

But apparently, that was not the case.

A WEEKEND OF SURPRISES

THE STUDENTS HAD TOLD ME I HAD BETTER STICK AROUND ON Saturday the 30th for an event. I did, even though it meant taking a pass on my chance to be a big star at the basketball game scheduled in Loja. ("I coulda been a contender!") After the last few weeks' games, I had even been invited by the opposing team to play with them at an away game down on the coast in Puerto Bolivar in July. Unfortunately, that area was out of my zone, and I would need permission to go.

At 2:30 a pick-up truck loaded with what looked like half the students from my classes, showed up at my place. They yelled "*Vámonos!*" ("Let's go!"), and we headed down to *Señor* Carrión's hacienda in the valley. The pick-up truck went into shuttle service mode and brought down the rest of the class members until all but six were there. It turned out that the event was for me! Padre Arias, as was his custom, started everybody off with a couple rounds of *trago* and made some welcoming remarks.

Lieutenant Ochoa, head of the military forces stationed near the airport (and my friend and member of the advanced class) made a very nice speech, specifically about me and about the Peace Corps in general. Then, on behalf of all three classes, he presented me with a plaque and certificate of appreciation. The certificate was signed by all the students from the three classes. The plaque, a bronze leaf on black enameled wood, read as follows:

"A keepsake from the students of the English night course, who salute their selfless professor, Mr. Gerardo Redfield, with the motive of celebrating Teachers Day on this esteemed day. In recognition of his unselfish labor for the benefit and cultural advancement of the people of Catamayo." I was overwhelmed by the sentiment and the gift and had trouble saying all I wanted to say about their effort, generosity and kindness, if not their stellar performance. I managed to apparently get out a few words of proper thanks and gratitude, as they all clapped, so I guess I managed to get the thought across. Or, perhaps they were just glad I'd finished and we could get on to the music and dancing. This music and dancing (and the drinking) went on for a good bit with an interruption for a buffet style dinner. Then more dancing and finally, at about 7:00, the fiesta finally broke up.

The "Big Surprise" was indeed a surprise as the National Teachers Day, as noted, had come and gone a couple of weeks earlier. After all the hours I put in on preparation, book acquisition, teaching, and correcting papers, it was really nice to be recognized for my effort. The plaque went on to find a prominent place on a shelf in the many homes in which I've lived over the years. These were good people, and whether I merited such glowing words is questionable. However, I did plant the seeds in a few for an education in English as a Second Language, and we had much fun in the process.

The week prior to my "big surprise" had been a busy one. I had finished my six-page case report on the project and sent that off in good time. I had been in and out of Loja, again in a quest to pick up the workers' pay, buy a bucket of nails and get a truck for a *minga* to haul rocks for pouring the floors. I heard that Justo Andrade was in town to accept an award for his twenty-five years of service and that he was planning a trip to Gonzanamá the following week. I wanted to talk with him, but we were not able to hook up.

When I came back from Loja, another surprise awaited me. I found out that one of my girls' teams had been invited to play in Gonzanamá on the following Sunday at a big area competition. The Director of the girls' school came to me and asked me if they should accept. I was even surprised to be asked, since I was just a coach. I told her it was fine with me and that they had shown improvement, but they would have to be willing to practice. And practice they did - all week, from 6:00 to 7:30 in the morning and 4:30 to 5:45 in the afternoon. I wasn't used to getting up at that hour, but if they were willing, so was I.

Sunday, May 31st was the date of the big games in Gonzanamá and the day after the "big surprise" fiesta. After partying the day before I was not in the best of shape, but we were to leave at 8:30 so there I was and so was "my" team. However, the Director heard that Justo was going to be passing through La Toma on his way to Gonzanamá, and she did not want to miss the chance to see him. She insisted on waiting to leave. I finally convinced her that there would be plenty of time to see and greet him when we got there. So, at 11:00 instead of 8:30, we finally got underway. A typical Ecuadorian start on the day.

We arrived in Gonzanamá at about 12:30 and were treated to a cold "hot lunch," and the girls headed down to practice and familiarize themselves with the court. After an hour and a half, they were very familiar with the court and eager to get underway. At 3:30, the Director finally came down to inform us that the girls couldn't play until the program to honor Justo was over. All the officials and people were there so they wouldn't be available to watch the game. Since these programs usually drone on for about two hours, at 4:30 we said (I said), "To hell with it." I told the girls to go out and do their warm up drills. We waited another forty minutes for the other team to show up. Finally, at about 5:50 the "friendship game" got underway, and my team was so hot under the collar and elsewhere that it was not their finest hour. My quick but short team went down to a resounding defeat against the "Amazon ladies" of Gonzanamá, some of whom were as tall as I was at five foot ten. The average height for Ecuadorian men was about five feet six inches, with the women being shorter.

After the game there was one more surprise in store for me. I finally got to talk to Justo. He told me he wanted me to move to Gonzanamá. They were going to start another school there, and he needed me to manage the project. He talked as if it was all a done deal and said that he had a letter from Smith for me in Loja.

Three surprises. From the heights to the depths all in one weekend. I had some work ahead of me.

MUCH TO CONSIDER

The following Monday I headed into Loja to once again see about lumber supplies, back pay, and most of all to see Justo about the letter from John Smith. I got the money for the workers and then went to see about the lumber that had been delaying progress on the roof. It appears that it had been there for five days, but people in charge could not agree on how much they were willing to pay a driver to haul it out to La Toma. "For want of a nail..." However, this time they promised it would be out that afternoon. Then Justo gave me the letter from John Smith.

The letter said, in effect, that Justo had talked over the move with him and that Smith was not opposed to it. He pointed out Justo was very enthusiastic about Gonzanamá as a site. "Well," I thought, "Justo may be but I'm not!" I was feeling very much at home in La Toma. As I said, I'd fallen in love with the town and the people. In spite of all my complaints, I was starting to feel like this was <u>my</u> town. I had friends, or at least, "regulars" I could trust, and my "go to" confidante, Marlene, with whom I could safely complain. As far as the Ecuadorian program leaders were concerned, I was probably just another piece on the chess board (I'm sure it was a pawn) that should be moved wherever needed. In their eyes my reluctance probably was viewed as me not being a good soldier. The only thing that made me even consider it was something that Smith had added: "Since Gonzanamá is only two hours away from La Toma, I could even envision you hanging on to your room in La Toma and commuting between both towns or at least getting back to La Toma at frequent enough intervals to keep your contacts there."

Smith's letter also mentioned that Justo might want me to accompany him on his trip to Gonzanamá on June 20th. I wasn't sure if I was to be introduced or to make the permanent move. I thought since I had my big, and approved, vacation plans for August, it would be ridiculous to move out there and then take off a month later. Some of the students in my English classes had also gotten wind of the potential move (maybe my confidante wasn't always so confidential!) and were talking about writing a letter to Smith asking that I be able to stay at least until we had finished the book, if not longer. However, since my English course was considered just a "sideline," I doubted how much weight that would carry. I decided to write Smith a letter myself asking about the June 20th move and see what he had to say. The proposed move would certainly put to rest any plans I had for projects after the school was finished.

As it turned out Smith came down to Loja the following week and we met over breakfast. I explained the vacation situation to him, and he asked me if I couldn't just change it to September. I explained to him I would be traveling with Ann and she had to be teaching classes by September. He suggested maybe going earlier. Then said he wasn't sure when they were going to get started in Gonzanamá anyway, and I should just keep going on in La Toma until I heard from him or Justo. He suggested if it happened, I could commute back to La Toma from time to time. When I pointed out the students wanting to complete the twelve lessons of the English book, he said maybe I could commute out of La Toma until that was done. That, I thought, would clearly be a hassle, given the on-again, off-again nature of the bus schedules and the fact that I would be bushed by the time I arrived. It was all clear as mud, and I was resigned to go into a "wait and see" mode. As I mentioned in a letter to my folks around this time, "I came back out on Monday morning and settled back into the rut." There seemed to be no incentive for the locals to start new things and nothing to do for me except work on finishing the current construction project, teach English, coach basketball, and plan for a trip around South America. In the meantime, I would do what I could to deal with day-to-day developments, and it was time for a trip to Quito for an annual physical.

...AND WHILE I WAS OUT

April, May and June, 1964

Politics:

- President Johnson, in a speech to a graduating class, presents his ideas for a "Great Society."
- Nelson Rockefeller beats Barry Goldwater in the Oregon Republican primary, slowing but not stalling Goldwater's march toward the nomination for president.
- California social conservatives, offended by Rockefeller's divorce and remarriage in 1963, choose Goldwater by a 3% margin, ensuring his nomination at the convention.
- Pennsylvania Governor William Scranton announces his candidacy for Republican presidential nomination as part of a "stop Goldwater effort."
- Barry Goldwater is one of six Republican senators voting against The Civil Rights Act.

Civil Rights:

- The Civil Rights Act is approved.
- The Supreme Court rules that closing schools to avoid desegregation is unconstitutional.
- Malcom X delivers what is considered the seventh most impactful speech of the Top 100 of the Century, "The Ballot

or the Bullet" in Cleveland, Ohio, advocating judicious voting by Blacks, and that failing, taking to arms.

- In Mississippi three Congress on Racial Equality (C.O.R.E.) members are abducted and murdered by White Knights of the Ku Klux Klan with the local police involved in the conspiracy.

Vietnam:

- Up to 1,000 students march in Times Square and 700 in San Francisco march in protest against the Vietnam War. Smaller but similar marches are held in Boston, Seattle, and Madison, Wisconsin.
- At a large demonstration in New York, New York, twelve men publicly burn their draft cards as a sign of resistance to the Vietnam war.
- The U. S. has 16,000 troops in Vietnam and 266 have been killed.
- General William Westmorland replaces General Paul Harkins and becomes head of U. S. forces in Vietnam.

International:

- The U. S. and Panama agree to resume diplomatic relations.
- President Johnson and Premier Nikita Khrushchev simultaneously announce plans to cut back on making materials for nuclear weapons.
- Growing strength of student power, demonstrations in Seoul, Korea, and eleven other cities drive the South Korean President to accept his right-hand man's resignation.
- South Korean President Park and his opposition leaders form a twenty-four member committee to resolve economic reforms in response to student demonstrations.

- Nelson Mandela and seven others are sentenced to life imprisonment and sent to Robben Island prison in South Africa.
- The last of France's military leaves Algeria.

Culture:

- Sidney Poitier becomes the first African-American to win the Academy Award for Best Actor in *Lilies of the Field.*

A TRIP TO QUITO

BEFORE I TOOK A TRIP TO QUITO FOR MY PHYSICAL AND SOME trip-planning, I wanted to make sure that things were solid at the work site. The lumber I had been promised a week ago still hadn't arrived so I went into Loja and found Joe Kelly sitting in his room reading a novel! Joe had pretty much bombed out on his Community Development efforts, so they assigned him to the School Construction Program basically as a scheduler and truck driver. However, he acted as if he had been put in charge of the whole program. I raised hell with him for the delay and talked him into loading the lumber onto the Peace Corps truck, and to bringing it out to La Toma. Then I went to check on the money that Justo said would be in last Monday as well and, of course, that hadn't arrived either. *Maestro* Ilescas owed about $300 to his workers for the work on the roof and plastering, and the money that was due in only amounted to $120. I was always in wonder how they continued working, but I guess employment for a national program was better than any other option available.

I stopped in to say goodbye to Bill Fuzetti, the engineer who had been assigned to the Loja Provincial Government and was heading home. He gave me some tips for making the trip around South America as he had done it previously. Bill was a really nice guy and one of the finest people I had met in my time in the Peace Corps. He had the right "can do" spirit and he had been very helpful over the last few months. I was going to miss him.

I returned to La Toma to make my flight reservations for Quito and to make a trip with the Padre to "influence" the brick maker. The Padre's presence added some much-needed pressure. The bricks had been promised for the last Saturday and then most recently for Wednesday. They weren't ready. This was the following Saturday, but they would be ready in <u>fifteen</u> days, we were told. As a result, I had to lay off two of the workers before I left. Not good for progress.

I was supposed to go out to Gonzanamá with Justo and Engineer Ruilloba, but they had not arrived when they were supposed to, so that issue remained unresolved before I left. As a final bit of preparation, I was fortunate enough to meet up with Len Guarderas in Loja. He was the son of the owner of the Guarderas Construction company, and he had just returned from four years of study in the U. S. at Purdue and Clemson Universities. He offered to substitute teach the English classes while I was in Quito. I thought it would be a great idea, so I put it to the vote of the students and they accepted his offer.

The trip for the annual physical event became somewhat of a class reunion with guys coming in at different times from all over the country. I flew up to Quito with Jim Snyder and the two Heifer Project Volunteers, Armond Joyce and Byron Bahl. Thursday and Friday were the check-up days and filled with the normal Peace Corps delays and waiting. While we waited around, this was our first chance to see what were relatively recent movies. After watching a steady diet of seven-year-old features in the flea infested theater in Loja, we made the best of seeing some that were only two to three years old. They included *One, Two, Three, 8 ½, The Fugitive Kind,* and *Never on Sunday*, which I had not seen before so that was "first run" for me.

The good news about my physical was that I was in good

shape except for some benign amoebas. Apparently, there are two kinds. You get both the same way, by eating food that has not been properly cleaned or is filled with infected water. Doc Caplin reminded me that I had better continue to be careful. Additionally, I made another trip to the dentist on that Friday to have a cavity filled that had been troubling me. Overall, I was glad to know that I was in relatively good shape compared to a number of others who had some major problems with "the bug."

I did some shopping for engagement and wedding rings as that was probably an expectation that would have to be met when Ann came down for vacation. The original plan was that she would be coming down with her mother, but I had made it pretty clear that if that were the case, it would be a two week rather than a four-week adventure. Once we determined that it would be a foursome with Joe and Pat Yoshida, we were back to the four-week plan. However, I suspected it was not without some fear and trepidation back home that her daughter would be "living in sin." (And what would the neighbors say?) The fact that her mother was no longer going to be a part of the trip certainly meant that there had better be some indication that "my intentions were honorable," so the ring purchase was an important part of that. Ann, I suspected, may have shared her mother's concern, but I hoped our letter writing would not have given her cause for alarm.

The "sizzling sixties" weren't at the boiling point that they were by the end of the decade, but they were simmering. Some unmarried couples were having premarital sex as they have had for centuries, but not openly. Girls/women who were known to do so were still thought of as "loose women" or "damaged goods." Guys who would "kiss and tell" could ruin a girl's reputation in an instant. So, it wasn't unusual for couples to wait until after marriage before having sex.

Bryon Bahl and I flew down to Guayaquil on the following Sunday. He and Jim Snyder and three other Heifer Project Volunteers were planning on making roughly the same loop, so we went from agency to agency and consulate to consulate to see what we could find. Our plan was to fly in a clockwise direction from Guyaquil to Trujillo, Peru to Iquitos, Peru, then on to Manaus, and Rio de Janerio, Brazil, down the east coast of the continent, through Argentina and then hop the Andes and come up the west coast through Chile, Peru and back to Guayaquil. Talks with Volunteers who had made the trip said the best and cheapest way was to make mostly internal flights in each country and use ground transportation to cross the borders. Most folks had done the loop at the time for around $600 to $700 (about $5,000 – $6,000 in today's value).

We found that the travel agencies had little interest in helping us with in-country flights as they made little or no profit on those. We went to the Ecuadorian Tours Agency, but they had nothing on Peruvian flights. So, on to the Peruvian consulate we went, and there we found a lovely little secretary and a gold mine of information. She called the Peruvian airlines and found out information on flights from Trujillo to Iquitos and how to achieve a $45.00 savings to get to Trujillo from Ecuador that involved river boats from Guayaquil to Puerto Bolivar, launches from there to another little town on the border, a walk across a bridge and a four-hour trip on a Greyhound type bus to Trujillo. That appeared to be an awful lot of messing around, but in 1964 it amounted to eight percent of the cost of the trip.

We went to the Brazilian consulate to get our tourist visas but were told they couldn't give them to us until we had proof of how we were to get out of the country. We also discovered that since the overthrow of Goulart in Brazil at the hands of the military (with a little U. S. help) the flight from Manaus to Rio had doubled. We decided to bite the bullet and make the reservations. By the end of the day, we had reservations made for the entire trip that included a bus ride from Sao Palo, Brazil, to Montevideo (to keep the Brazilians happy about our exit) and a means of seeing La Paz, Bolivia, and Lake Titicaca on the way back to Peru. All that for less than $600.

Not a bad day's work. And now it was time to get back to my real work.

BACK AT THE RANCH

WHILE I WAS IN GUAYAQUIL WITH BYRON AND JIM SNYDER, I had run into two other Volunteers, one of whom had success in getting four separate communities to pull together and work to assemble the required amount of sand, rocks, gravel and lumber to prove to the School Construction Program officials that they were serious about doing their part. He was then informed that the Program at the government level only had enough money to pay for one of the communities. He had lost all credibility and had to get out of there to escape the ire of the people before they all but lynched him. So, when Engineer Ruilloba arrived in La Toma to check on progress, I was not surprised when he made no mention of Gonzanamá. I suspected the Program was, indeed, in trouble. It would explain the multiple number of times we had to wait for payment for supplies and workers.

My suspicions were confirmed when Smith came through town while taking a couple of new Volunteer teachers to towns down the road. He said he was going to talk to Justo about the situation in Gonzanamá and whether they had enough money to fund it, when it might be started, etc. He concluded that if the School Construction Program was in financial trouble, I could stay in La Toma if I could get some of the projects started that we had discussed. However, he wouldn't be blaming me if they didn't as he thought I was a "pretty live wire." I guess that was his way of saying I had done my best to get things going and wasn't just dogging it. Smith added that there were plenty of other places and projects where I could go if things didn't work out here in La Toma. He then told me that he was finishing up in August, going home to Minnesota, and we would be dealing with a new Representative. More uncertainty was just what I didn't need at this point, but I had no control over the outcome.

I grabbed a ride into Loja with Smith to retrieve a dresser that I bought from Bill Fuzetti. It had been a long, drawn-out saga (which I've spared you) that ran over three months of trying to have one built in Loja that fortunately ended with me getting my money back. So, I was glad to take advantage of the opportunity to get Bill's. I just had to figure a way to get it out to La Toma in order to end six months of using my footlocker and cot for a dresser. When I got to Bill's old apartment, the one which Joe Kelly had taken over, it was locked. Joe was in Quito with the key. I almost turned blue with frustration and was ready to return to La Toma when Jim Snyder showed up with a key and reminded me that it was the Fourth of July.

We caught a movie and then joined Armond Joyce and Bill White to at least make an effort to salute the Fourth in a proper manner. As luck would have it, the next day the Guarderas soccer team was in town for a game, and my now good friend Juvenal came over with one of their trucks. We hauled the dresser out to La Toma, and I spent the rest of the afternoon finally completely unpacking my duffel bag and footlocker and giving myself a right and proper dresser. After seven months, I had finally "settled in." The question remained, "How long would I stay?"

Doug Strauss stopped by on his way back from Quito and told me he had talked with Justo while there. He told me that Justo, two big USAID bosses, and the Minister of Education would be down here on July 15th to arrange for the inauguration (dedication) here and to inaugurate some schools that had already been finished. Doug informed me that Justo wanted this school to be inaugurated by August 15th. I thought, "If they want it finished by then, they had better free up some dollars so we could make it happen." And, if it was to be inaugurated on that date, I would be in the middle of my trip around South America. If it was conducted anything like the last time they came through, my absence would have the same effect as taking one's finger out of a bowl of water. These were usually such long winded affairs, with everyone praising the other for their wonderful cooperation, when the reality was that they had practically been at each other's throats to get things to happen for the previous nine to ten months. I would not miss it a bit, other than to make sure the workers were recognized at this one. They were usually ignored as the inaugurations happened long after they were gone.

WRAPPING UP

My trip with Ann was about two weeks away, and I was trying to get everything I could in place. First, I had to do some of my "official" duties. It was graduation time for the schools. I didn't think I had anything to do with it, but I was informed that the local "dignitaries" usually attend. I had missed one ceremony, and that's how I found that I was considered one of those notables. I attended the rest.

The students have open oral exams, which actually don't go on their records or mean anything as far as passing or failing. It keeps the parents happy and gives the kids a chance to show off their knowledge and display some of the things they had made during the year. These all-day events last for four days straight. Teachers from other schools come in to judge the students and even grade the individual teachers on their performances. I was invited to the girls' school on Thursday, which was the one that I had previously missed in my ignorance of my local "status." On Friday I attended ceremonies at the boys' school and on Saturday another at the parochial school.

Sunday was the day for the sixth-grade graduation ceremonies. For the majority of the students, this would be the end of their formal education. Others would be destined for high schools in Loja or elsewhere depending on their economic situation. The two sixth grade classes lined up on the basketball court, said what I assumed to be a pledge of allegiance to the flag, gave an oath of some sort and then each came forward, knelt and kissed the flag. That was it for the ceremony. What followed were a series of skits, orations or dance performances by the students and then a chaperoned dance with a record player and ample amounts of *trago* for the parents and "dignitaries".

We held what I hoped would be our last *minga* to get more rocks and, with the help of the military recruits and the police, we managed to get twelve truckloads hauled. The school was looking good with half of the tiles in place on the roof. On his own authority, Engineer Ruilloba had approved the addition of a principal's office, which usually required approval from much higher ups. He liked what we had done. It only lacked 200 bricks for completion. To no one's surprise, the bricks were not ready.

Padre Arias stands among (and on) rocks donated for construction.

I made a run into Loja for a number of reasons, but the primary goal was to price materials for some playground equipment, something they never had in La Toma. I also had to get the final lumber order for the roof. I did that, found a truck, and had the stuff shipped out to La Toma.

While in Loja I also met with Ruilloba who wanted me to meet with the Point-4 bosses from Quito who had come down for some inaugurations, which included one in Cangonamá. The Point-4 was a program started under Harry Truman to offer U. S. "know how" and technical assistance to underdeveloped countries and, broadly speaking, the school construction effort was under that umbrella. Specifically, as mentioned, it was under Kennedy's Alliance for Progress. He wanted me to get him off the hook for independently approving the addition of the principal's office. The Point-4 bosses and Justo had left before I had a chance to do so. But there was to be another opportunity.

I also had some goodbyes to say; one of them was to John Smith, who was leaving August 1st, and the other was a surprise - a goodbye to Joe Orr. When I arrived at the apartment Joe was packing, and gave me the news that he and Pat had decided to get married. Since the big chiefs would not allow Pat to transfer here, Joe was transferring to Colombia. That would put a kink in our joint vacation plans, but I was happy for them. Pat was still coming down to Quito at the end of the month, and they would tie the knot as soon as possible. They would then take their vacation as a honeymoon, and Joe said they could meet us in Chile. He was planning on being in Quito when I arrived there at the end of the month, so I made plans to look him up, or rather look them up, when I got there.

While I was helping Joe take his trunks to the bus station, Hugo, Padre Reyes' helper from our first assignment in Cangonamá, approached me. He said that they were going to have an inauguration of that school the following Tuesday, and they wanted me to come up and take part. Since that was my first assignment, I accepted.

That Tuesday I caught a bus out of La Toma at 9:00 and got to Playas. Hugo was also on the bus, and he had arranged to have the local "rent a mule" waiting for me. After I talked him into riding half way and me walking half way, we finally left. He didn't know what to make of me. I think he had been a servant so long he couldn't get used to the idea of him riding and me walking but, in that manner, we made it up to the school by 3:00. That was the time that Justo and the biggies were supposed to arrive but this was Ecuador, 1964. They arrived at 5:00, and the festivities got underway. I got my chance to talk to the Point-4 boss, Don Peterson, who was sitting in for Watson. I think I got Ruilloba off the hook for approving the additional work by explaining that we received additional contributions of work and materials at the local level to make it possible.

We had the usual buffet, and then I hooked a ride back with Justo at about 8:00. We were ambushed by a group of school kids when we got to Catacocha. They were there to receive the Secretary of Education who was part of our entourage, and they insisted we stay for their ceremonies. We had to sit through speeches and presentations and petitions for new schools and rooms to be built there. Then we went to dinner once again. I took advantage of this time to talk to Justo and let him know that I was not in favor of moving to Gonzonamá, but that I would be glad to monitor the progress from La Toma. I argued that if things didn't pan out in La Toma by September, then I would reconsider. He said that was okay with him. I don't know if it was the hour of the day, the financial problems, or my logic, but for the moment that problem was solved. Now it was time to get ready for my vacation.

THE BEST LAID PLANS

My bags were packed, and I was off on the first leg of a long month of travel. As the bank robber said, "I had it all figured out, except for the police." Things do not always go as planned. It was July 29th, and I was actually leaving earlier than scheduled. Ann's plane was arriving two days earlier than I stated in my Peace Corps communication, and I had to be there to meet her. I checked into the last room available at my favorite hotel, the Hotel Colón, and had dinner with Joe Orr who, as it turned out, was NOT getting married. Twelve hours before Pat and he were ready to tie the knot, the Quito Peace Corps office received a letter from Washington refusing permission for them to do so. It was a shocker. All the Colombian and Ecuadorian arrangements they had made and the expenses arranging for the wedding went down the drain. Joe sent off a strong but well-written letter to Frank Mankiewicz, who headed up the Latin American Peace Corps, asking him to reconsider but heard nothing. The upshot for us was that Ann and I were back to having the travel companions we had originally arranged. However, their travel plans hadn't been made with the same itinerary as were ours.

Ann's plane got in on time, and I took her to the hotel so she could get some rest in the room she would share with Pat. I went to the Peace Corps offices where I ran into John Smith. Scratching his chin, he asked, "Aren't you up here a little early?" I explained that Ann's arrival had been moved up two days. This was true; however, the decision had been made by us three months ago. And, I thought, "You're leaving, anyway." However, his work was not quite finished.

He informed me that the Ecuadorian government had just received a five million dollar loan from the United States for the School Construction Program, and Justo really wanted me on the Gonzanamá job. Smith felt I ought to take it. I thought it over for a while and, after obtaining his assurance that I could stay in La Toma, I agreed to do so. He also told me that the Peace Corps would pay for extra lodging in Gonzanamá and cover my transportation costs. That made it pretty hard to say no. We tried to confirm these plans by calling Justo but he was out. I was told he would call me back the next morning.

In the afternoon, Ann and I went over to the Peace Corps office for a depressing "un-wedding" party that had been set up by Bob Carey and Toni Crossi. They were another engaged couple that evolved during the Albuquerque training. Toni was scheduled to room with Ann before she had to drop out, so they were already good friends. We ate the wedding cake, broke open the bottles of champagne, and then went to dinner at the Hotel Florida where a number of other Volunteers were staying. Although the facilities were not quite as nice as the Colón, the daily rate was 20 per cent less and included meals. We moved there the next day.

In the morning I went to the office again and waited for the call from Justo, which never came. I said my goodbyes again to John Smith and headed downtown to the jeweler to pick up the rings I had ordered and got a haircut. I was prepared for the big event.

We two couples did the tourist bit and went downtown in the afternoon. Joe told us about a flight he had checked out and that called for a change of our plans. I've noted before that the Brazil trip had doubled in price, and there was a four-day delay in getting out of Manaus, Brazil. Since time was of the essence, we went with Joe's plan. The move saved money, eliminated about 4,000 travel miles, and got us right into Lima. So, our flight plan was now changed. We would depart Quito on August 3rd for Lima, Peru, spend three days there, and then on to Cuzco, Peru, for two days. We would fly from Cusco to La Paz, Bolivia, and on to Buenos Aires and environs for seven days. We would hop a flight to Santiago, Chile, and the Chilean coast for seven days. Our plans were to backtrack to La Paz and Lima for two days each, show the girls the wonders of Guayaquil for two more days, and wrap up with a return to Quito on August 29th. We picked up our tickets, acquired a very detailed travel guide, and I submitted my required itinerary to the office.

That night I took Ann to dinner at the Colón. By the alchemy of a quiet atmosphere, soft music, a little wine and an excellent meal I emerged not only full but engaged. I'm not sure what motivated my comments in sending the news to my parents - youthful, macho sarcasm or perhaps uncertainty, but they read as follows: "Well, last night I put my head in the noose, but at least it's a while before the trapdoor springs. I think I'm a victim of the Tender Trap." The song, "The Tender Trap," was popular at that time and said in part, "*...you're hooked, you're cooked, you're caught in the tender trap.*" And, so I was. Ann had a ring on her finger. She was thrilled, and I'm sure her mother was much relieved as well. The next day we celebrated with a trip to the "center of the world," the equator marker which lies about fourteen miles north of Quito.

I'll spare you the details of the tourism part of the trip. You can get the highlights of each city from any travel show, book, or brochure. We saw more than our share of gold encrusted

Here I am at the Equator, with one foot in the Southern Hemisphere and one foot in the Northern.

churches and cathedrals; tombs of the famous heroes; government buildings and monuments; and a number of beautiful parks. As one might suspect, all did not go as planned, and I'll share just a few of the anomalies with you that I hope capture some of our experience. Other than flight plans, we had planned to "play the trip by ear" in the fine, flexible fashion of the Peace Corps Volunteer. That backfired immediately. When we arrived in Lima on August 3rd, we discovered that all the hotels in Cuzco were booked until the 17th. We shifted our itinerary the first day out and decided to make the loop in a counter clockwise direction: Chile, Argentina, Uruguay, Bolivia, Peru and back to Ecuador. We spent most of the first day in Lima rearranging flights and confirming our flights to Arequipa, Peru, and Santiago, Chile. We did the Peace Corps shuffle, flying first to Arequipa where, to our surprise, we found that their beautiful churches, made of white volcanic stone, had been destroyed in a 1960 earthquake. Most were still under reconstruction. The next day we flew to Tacna, a town about 35 miles from the Chilean border. We then took a train out of Tacna to Arica, Chile. We had reserved tickets for a jet from Arica to Santiago (a 1,400 mile trip for only $20), but had to confirm when we got there. Our revised plan was to "do" Chile: Santiago, Valpara*íso* and Viña del Mar, Concepción and Los Lagos, the lake region. Then we would head back to Santiago and hop over by air to Buenos Aires and Montevideo. From there it was on to La Paz, Bolivia, and Cuzco, Peru, (where we hoped the hotels would have more accommodations), and then to Lima and back. Most of those plans played out as scheduled except for the Los Lagos area.

After living in blue jeans, work shirts and boots for a year, it was quite a shift for Joe and me to be wearing white shirts and ties on the trip. Pat and Ann generally wore low heeled pumps and skirts for most of our travels. During this era, if one was traveling by air, you dressed for the occasion. The days of backpacks and jeans and sneakers travel attire would have to await the seventies.

Ann and I flew down to Concepción and had dinner at a country club with a young woman who had been an exchange student in my home town a few years after I had left. She and her boyfriend were about our age, very cosmopolitan and sophisticated. I marveled at how she had dealt with our small-town culture. They gave us the grand tour of the city, and the next day Ann and I enjoyed a bus ride through the beautiful Chilean countryside back up to Santiago. We decided we would save Los Lagos for another day far in the future. When we got to Santiago we unexpectedly ran into "*Lojanos*" Jim Snyder, Armond Joyce and Mary Ann Mobley at our hotel. Small world - we had an impromptu Ecuadorian Volunteer convention!

The next day we left for Buenos Aires, a city of almost three million people - quite a contrast to the adobe walled churches and buildings of Quito and Loja! Santiago was big, but Buenos Aires reminded me of being in New York. We didn't spend much time there as our plane was two hours late arriving. We spent the first night at multiple agencies trying to figure the cheapest and quickest way out of there to La Paz. The cheapest was by train, but that was a four-day trip. We ended up settling on a flight for August 18th that left once a week. It was an international flight and the most expensive of the entire trip, eighty-three dollars for passage on a DC-3. We also took time to make arrangements for a round-trip ticket on a boat to Montevideo.

The trip to Montevideo, Uruguay, was a nightmare from the start. First, our boat trip left three hours late on Saturday the 15th, so we didn't get into the city until 9:30 at night. We discovered that the 15th was the date of a big cattleman's convention, and the 17th was the birthday of José de San Martin, the liberator of Chile, Argentina, and Peru. It was a national holiday in Buenos Aires, just across the bay. As a result, every good hotel in Montevideo was full. We rode around in a taxi for almost three hours, proud at first, rejecting the flea bags we encountered. Finally, tired and dejected, we took a place that was probably much worse than the first few we had turned down. In the morning we tried again at decent hotels, hoping somebody had checked out but with no luck. We resigned ourselves to taking a taxi tour of the city and then caught a bus which took us to the boat back to Buenos Aries. "Seasoned world travelers" that we had become, we now wired ahead for reservations.

The next day we took the grand tour of Buenos Aires. The city is a shopping mecca and we did our share, but we did more window shopping than purchasing. The city was and is a very expensive place, and our hotel was right next to the Calle Florida, the Rodeo Drive or Michigan Avenue of Buenos Aires, not the place for people on a Peace Corps budget, to say the least. We capped off the day at a restaurant in the Italian part of this very European-like city.

Then it was on to La Paz where we had originally planned to spend two days. However, when I got off the plane it felt like I was walking on the deck of a ship. Joe was having the same problem. The elevation of La Paz is over 11,900 feet, and we were feeling the effects of that in a big way. Ann promptly got sick, and it was a rough night all the way around. We decided to beat feet out of there the next day. We left La Paz at 2:00 in the afternoon, and by 6:00 we were at the shores of Lake Titicaca, the highest navigable fresh water lake in the world. Its elevation is even higher than La Paz, but there was not the level of pollution that seemed to cover that city.

Unfortunately, the old passenger boat that was to carry us across the lake did not leave until 10:30 that night which meant we would not make our train connection in Puño, Peru, the next morning. Picture in your mind a sort of a large version of the "African Queen" but with room for lodging. Ann and Pat went to sleep in their bunks but Joe and I spent the entire night on the boat playing cards with a Maryknoll priest who regaled us with his stories of missionary activities in Bolivia as we chugged all the way across the lake.

What <u>was</u> available in Puño the next morning was a train with one passenger car connected to an old steam engine that probably should have been in a museum, but that's what took us to Cuzco. We left at 9:00, slowly winding our way through the Andes and finally reaching Cuzco at 10:30 that evening. Although the elevation of Cuzco is only a little lower than La Paz, our bodies had apparently adjusted to the altitude. We had an excellent guide, an archeology student at the university who really knew his stuff about Cuzco, the ancient capital of the Incas, and Machu Picchu. We truly enjoyed the sites and his expertise.

We closed the loop by flying to Lima and then on to Guayaquil. In Guayaquil who should we run into but Gerry Mussett! He had found employment on the SS Hope, the charitable hospital ship that was providing services in the harbor. He had kept in touch with the Volunteers and told Joe that the scuttle butt was that their marriage had now been approved. So, we all flew up to Quito and, after the usual amount of Ecuadorian red tape, Pat and Joe were finally married, exactly one month later than planned. We wished them well and sent them on their way to Colombia.

The next day, Ann and I bid our tearful goodbyes. She left for the States to plan our wedding, and I left for Cuenca to meet with Justo Andrade. It was time to seal the deal on Gonzanamá.

PART IV

A SOFT RE-ENTRY

I MET WITH JUSTO IN CUENCA ON SEPTEMBER 2ND, AND WE HAD a fairly good discussion about the Gonzanamá project. It would be different, as the plan was to build it with cement blocks, made on the site, using a small motor driven machine. "No more waiting for the brickmaker - probably now waiting for the cement to arrive," I thought to myself. Justo was still unhappy that I was not moving permanently to Gonzanamá, but I had won that battle with Smith which he acknowledged. However, he wanted me down there four to five days a week in the coming month of October as they were just in the "gathering stage," pulling together the promised local contribution of sand, rocks and gravel that had to be on site before work could commence. I agreed to do so, but we also agreed the important thing now was to ready the La Toma school for the inauguration. It had not taken place in my absence, and I was glad of that. In truth, it would be nice to be there after all I had been through, acknowledged or not.

Justo offered me a ride from Cuenca to Loja with Engineer Ruilloba who was leaving the next afternoon. The next day, I waited for his arrival, but true to my experiences with offered rides with this outfit, he never came. I ended up taking a 7:00

p.m. bus down to Loja along with George Bennett, who had taken Joe Orr's place in Zamora and at the apartment. We didn't arrive there until 4:00 a.m., but we could not get into the apartment because George had lent his keys to Wally Benson. Wally had left them at the Alaska to be picked up. Of course, at this hour it was closed. I hadn't taken my keys on the trip, as I planned to return directly to La Toma, so I was of no help. We checked into a hotel for what was left of the night.

George got up well before me the next morning. He left the hotel, went to the Alaska, got the keys, proceeded to the apartment, changed and left - with the keys. So, I schlepped my baggage over to Jim Snyder's place only to find he wasn't home. I crawled through a window to gain entry. I knew Jim would not mind since he was such a cool headed and accommodating guy.

Later in the day I talked with Engineer Ruilloba who apologized for not getting the message about bringing me down from Cuenca. He said he would be out to inspect the school the next day on his way to Macar*á* and Joe Kelly would come out and take me to Gonzanamá so we could meet with the school construction committee there on Saturday.

I finally reached La Toma that evening, and I was "home" again after thirty-two days. Most everyone seemed very happy to see me. A lot of them said they thought that I had deserted them for good and I wasn't coming back. Marlene, in particular, seemed a bit more distant. (Maybe she had expected a post card?) There was a change in the dynamic that I couldn't put my finger on, but perhaps it was just my being away. The pace of activity up to the point of my departure, in spite of the delays, had been pretty intense - at least for me. Now we were down to the final strokes and maybe that was it.

Ruilloba and I went to inspect the La Toma school, and it was quite well along. All that remained was to put in the ceilings, doors, windows and, finally, the plumbing. I suspected that the plumbing might take some time given the water situation in town, but it was to be plumbed. Ruilloba seemed very pleased, and we agreed to meet later in the day in Gonzanamá. I spent the remainder of the day waiting for Joe Kelly to show up. He was supposed to arrive at about 2:00 but never came. Had I known he was not coming I could have taken a 1:00 bus and made the meeting. The next bus was at 5:30, which would have gotten me there much too late. What a great start for my work in Gonzanamá.

I decided to go into Loja on Monday to find out what happened with Joe. I had another reason to be there as well. When I had opened the door to my room in La Toma on Friday evening, I was greeted by quite a sight. Temporary tenants, rats or mice, had strewn the innards of my mattress all over the place. That was my welcome home. I cleaned up the mess and slept on the cot, but that was not going to be a permanent situation. I needed to buy a new mattress.

The good news was that I had plenty of time for such activities as my re-entry came at a time that basically gave me another week of vacation. It was the week of the celebration of the Patron Saint of the Province of Loja, the Virgin of El Cisne. The town of El Cisne is the site of a huge white basilica, modeled after one in Harlungenberg, Germany, that looms above the whitewashed adobe buildings that surround it. The Ecuadorian legend is that in 1594, when they finished a six-foot tall image of the Virgin Mary modeled after the one in Guadalupe, Mexico, and brought it from Quito to El Cisne, she created a rainstorm that ended a major drought. It was deemed a miracle, and people have been making pilgrimages to the site ever since. The Virgin is carried from El Cisne, in a three-day, 40-mile procession to Loja on August 17th. Starting on September 8th there is a week-long "International" Fair celebrating the event. It is considered international because there is also participation from Colombian and Peruvian merchants who come into town, and the contraband restrictions are down for that week. The statue of the Virgin Mary stays in Loja until November 3rd when the procession returns to El Cisne. I mention this, as it had implications for things to come. The *Maestro* took the whole week off to go up to El Cisne with his family and then back to Cuenca. The other workers had left as well. So, I had some time to recover from our trip.

I stayed in Loja for a couple of days. I purchased a new canteen at the Fair and then met with Mike Aguirre, the Rep who had replaced John Smith. He took back my passport (the device by which they prevented unauthorized travel), and offered me a new book locker and said he would get me an English record to assist with my classroom efforts. I was impressed with Mike. Outgoing and affable, it seemed like he would be a good guy to replace Smith. I returned with my new mattress and chose to use these free days to catch up on overdue correspondence and a little home improvement. I was going to build a bookcase but discovered the wood I had was not suitable. Instead, I constructed new shelving for my "kitchen" area which I then covered with oil cloth. I even had some left over for my desk. Now I had pink and green walls and red gingham shelves. At least the place was colorful.

In my hunt for projects, I had checked out the cost of playground items and had passed that information on to the playground committee before I left on vacation. While I was gone, the committee had cooled on that idea due to lack of contributions, but they now wanted to get going on an effort to get a new water system built. (Remember, we had run out of water during the *minga* when we were pouring the beam.) Previously Suco and I, along with John Mulligan, the Volunteer engineer working with the Municipal government, had checked out an old well behind the commercial area of town. Mulligan said that he believed there was more water there. By digging a long deep trench, we could find more, and with a pump, tubes and a tank placed on top of one of the surrounding hills, we could serve the whole dry part of the upper valley.

In this "down" week I checked out some of the other local wells with Ruben Patiño who had become my closest local friend. He was one of my best English students, the son of a local merchant, a good sketch artist, and one of the few who had invited me into his home for dinner. Energetic and wanting to be part of the process, he had a lot of ideas for improving the community but took a dim view of some of the prospects for their completion given his experience with a lot of big talkers and no action. We looked at a number of wells in another attempt to determine which would be the best candidate for creating a new water tank to serve this very dry area of upper La Toma. It turned out that the well Suco and I had looked at before was still the top candidate.

I got into a discussion with Ruben and his father about a proposed canal project that had previously been discussed but had not come to fruition. I thought that would perhaps be a very good candidate for a community development effort. Ruben asked me if I would like to take a hike along the proposed route and see where the dam that would create it would be built. The area was locally known as the "Bridge of the Incas," as the story was that it was on the ancient Incan trail from Cuzco to Quito. This sounded like a good idea to see an historic site that might even become a tourist attraction. And, I had the time available.

With my new canteen in hand, Ruben, Miguel Montaño, one of the teachers (Julio Garcia, if I recall correctly), and I set out at about at 8:30 on Sunday morning. We walked and walked and walked - first over hills, then up mountains, down into valleys, and finally through thick brush, arriving around 3:00 at the river which could be dammed to provide the water for the canal. We kept going and did not get to the Bridge of the Incas until 5:30. The plan was to cross the river, which led to a road and another bridge we would have to cross in order to catch the bus back to La Toma. As I looked across the river at the stone abutments that once held the timbers and ropes of the bridge. I noted, much to my disappointment, that there were round iron rings that had once supported the ropes. The Incas had copper and bronze in their day but no iron. In my mind, we had trudged this far for nothing, and my expectation of it becoming a big discovery or tourist attraction were dashed. And there were more disappointments ahead.

The river was too high and impossible to cross at that point. We had to walk about another five miles down-river to another spot where we could safely cross. After stripping to our skivvies

Ruben, Julio García and Miquel Montaño take a much-needed break during our trek to the Bridge of the Incas.

and crossing the river, we reached the road at about 7:00. The bus we had hoped to catch came by just three minutes later. It was full and passed right by. We set out again and were ultimately and thankfully picked up by a passing truck that took us into La Toma where we arrived, tired and exhausted, at 8:30 that night. And Ruben was (and is) still my friend! It was pretty clear to me why no one had attempted to bring the canal to La Toma. I didn't mention that to Ruben, and I never heard any more about that possibility during my time there.

No water to be had from that source. However, later that week I did take a sample from the well we had selected into Loja to have it analyzed. It would take another week to get results.

BACK AT IT

THE *MAESTRO* AND HIS CREW RETURNED THE NEXT WEEK, AND things seemed to be back in somewhat of a routine. My English classes were significantly reduced in size as the Guarderas people were almost finished with the La Toma area of the Pan-Am Highway, and most had moved into Loja. I decided to keep the two half-hour sessions with the first group and tutor the second class as they finished the book on their own. I figured with my potential move or commute to Gonzanamá, I wouldn't be able to prepare and teach two hours of classes anyway.

The painters arrived at the school and went right at it. They first put on a coat of white, and I thought it was finished. They then proceeded to do a patchwork of purple, yellow and a pink on alternating bricks. It was a color riot! I don't know who ordered or authorized it, but it was certainly eye catching. Doors were being hung but still needed varnish and hardware. The *maestro* and his crew were putting in the wrought iron windows, and another crew of carpenters had put up most of the ceilings in the first building.

I made a couple of attempts to get to Gonzanamá by bus when not attending to the school, but every time I tried, the buses were full. Ruilloba was due in the following week, and I figured we would go down together and make up for my absence while he was present. I wrapped up re-entry week with a trip to Loja to attend a farewell party for Doug Strauss who was leaving for a new assignment in Cuenca. One of his Loja pals prepared the invitations, so it was quite the social affair with many of the big-name families of Loja represented but very few of our gang. Doug had done well in that sense. I was glad to have been invited, but now I was the only one left from the Cangonamá immersion. What I had considered "my gang" (Doug, Joe, and Gerry) had all shipped out and I was feeling a bit adrift. There were still plenty of Volunteers left in the Loja area, but none who had the experiences the four of us had in common.

A view from my apartment building balcony of major improvements being made to the Pan-Am Highway that ran through the town.

Engineer Ruilloba and I left from Loja together the following Monday and headed to Gonzanamá and on to another little town, Quilanga, where they were frantically working to finish a school that was to be inaugurated on the following Saturday. To make sure that the school was ready, Ruilloba borrowed *Maestro* Illescas and two of his helpers and took them along with us. We returned to Gonzanamá that night and met with the school inspector. He said we would probably have quite a time there since the town was divided up into factions and not too many people were willing to help. Most of the *mingas* were being done by people from nearby barrios.

The inspector went on to inform us that some of the people wanted to start digging trenches for the foundation on the upcoming Saturday, but there was hardly any material there to put in it. They had about six truckloads of stone and three truckloads of sand. The requirement was to have on hand a hundred truckloads of each. Ruilloba told him he wanted at least a quarter of that requirement met and materials on sight before we started anything. I would have felt better knowing half was on site, but he wanted to be accommodating. It was a good thing that the buses in La Toma had been filled the previous week because I probably would have told them to call me when the 100 truckloads were on site and offended the whole bunch. The inspector said that all the people do in Gonzanamá is pass their time cutting up one another behind each other's back. I had had a hunch about this town, and it looked like there was a real challenge ahead. We talked a little about getting me a room, and he said he thought he could find me one. We left it at that.

I again had real reservations about going down there, given the situation, but the Program was committed to going ahead, and I was part of the "package." With people so divided and at each other's throats (or backs), the odds on getting anything else started of a developmental nature seemed slim to none. And, in truth, I had nothing solid to show in La Toma to indicate I needed to stay there. I had ideas: a library, a water project, a remedial literacy program that had just come to mind, and the Centro Cultural's new building to be built with our idle Cinva-Ram machine. For the moment they were all "pie in the sky."

...AND WHILE I WAS OUT

July, August and September, 1964

Politics:

- President Johnson signs the Civil Rights Act of 1964.
- Republican candidate Nelson Rockefeller is booed extensively when he denounces extremism.
- The U. S. Congress approves the Gulf of Tonkin Resolution by a margin of 416 to 0 in the House and 88 to 2 in the Senate, giving President Johnson extensive war powers and avoiding a declaration of war.
- Barry Goldwater declares that "extremism in the defense of liberty is no vice" and that "moderation in the pursuit of justice is no virtue" and gains the nomination for president on the first ballot at the Republican National Convention.
- President Johnson's campaign airs the controversial "Daisy" ad featuring a little girl and a huge mushroom cloud suggesting a Goldwater victory would lead to nuclear war.
- University of California, Berkeley's Dean of Students issues an order banning the use of posters, easels and tables on campus, and around twenty student organizations form a coalition to oppose the regulations proposed by the Dean. (This will result in the formation of "The Free Speech Movement.")

- The Warren Commission Report is released concluding that Oswald alone killed JFK and sets off a number of conspiracy theories by disbelievers.

Civil Rights:

- The Civil Rights Act of 1964 becomes law.
- Six days of rioting begins in Harlem.
- Jesse Grey, the leader of a rent strike, calls for 100 skilled black revolutionaries to "correct the police brutality in Harlem."
- Race riots erupt in Patterson and Elizabeth, New Jersey, and Philadelphia. Forty-one people are injured; seven hundred and forty-four people are arrested in Philadelphia.
- A black delegation at the Democratic National Convention, The Mississippi Freedom Democratic Party, led by Fannie Lou Hammer, challenges the seating of the all-white delegation from Mississippi. They are not seated.
- Freedom Summer in Mississippi draws to a close. There have been thirty-five shooting incidents, six murders of activists, eighty beatings, and sixty-five churches and houses burned.
- On California's Berkeley campus, organized activist civil rights students picket *The Oakland Tribune*, the newspaper owned by U. S. Senator William Knowland.

Vietnam:

- U. S. Military Personnel announce that U. S. casualties in Vietnam are 1,387 with 399 dead and seventeen MIA.
- The U. S. sends 5,000 more military advisors to South Vietnam, bringing the total to 21,000.
- General Nguyen Khanh, in a U. S. backed coup, becomes the Chief of State in South Vietnam and institutes a new constitution, drafted in part by the U. S. Embassy.

- In Saigon, mob violence erupts after students and Buddhist militants protest against Khanh's U. S. backed regime.

International:

- Malawi declares its independence from Britain.
- The former Belgian Congo changes its name to the Democratic Republic of the Congo.
- Malta becomes independent from Britain.

Culture:

- *Mary Poppins* has its world premiere, becoming Disney's biggest money maker and garnering five Academy Awards.
- *Shindig*, a musical variety show replaces *Hootenanny*, a program on ABC that featured folk music. Later TV shows air from London featuring the Beatles and other groups of the "British Invasion."

READING & WRITING & ???

I HAD BAD NEWS AND GOOD NEWS THE FOLLOWING WEEK WITH my search for projects that would improve the wellbeing of La Toma. The results from the bottle of water from the well that I took to Loja for testing came back with negative results (in layman's terms). In medical terms, it came back with positive results for being full of amoebas and intestinal parasites. So that was the bad news. If there was to be a water project, it certainly was not going to be from this source, the well we thought to be the top candidate. On the good news side, I received a telegram inviting me to attend a course for teaching literacy that was being offered in Loja the following Friday and Saturday. I decided to attend.

The other project I was working toward was establishing a library, a project that I thought about when I got the CARE brochures and booklets a while back. When I was in Cuenca for my meeting with Justo, I talked with Volunteer Gil Hall, who had received help from his hometown when he wrote to tell them of the lack of money for a library in his town. They had responded with over $400 in contributions, and he and his committee worked to get books at a cut rate through their Cultural Center. I ran the idea by Luis Garcia, and he was very excited about it. He even said that when Carlos Carrión and his family moved out to a new place, which they were building at that time, we could probably use their space. People could refurbish the room and donate furniture and books. That sounded great. The question was, "Who do I write back home?" (Or, "to whom?") In a letter to my mother, still an active English teacher at my old high school, I asked for her thoughts on the matter.

When I went into Loja on Thursday, I was supposed to meet with Justo but, since the course started the next day, he thought I would still be in La Toma, and he was out making a big loop around the territory. Now the likelihood of our meeting would probably take another two weeks. I didn't know if I dodged a bullet or just missed a meeting, but I was glad to have another couple of weeks to find out. I had an ulterior motive in attending the literacy course.

On Friday the sponsors, who were from CARE, presented the course outline. It was a two-part process. The first course was for adults who never learned to read and emphasized the importance of how to deal with them in a sensitive manner. This course would probably be taught by Luis Garcia from the La Toma faculty. Frankly, as important as it was, I was not interested in teaching that one. It was the second course that held some potential for my efforts to stay in town.

The second course was for those people who were taught how to read and write but had forgotten most of what they had learned. They were deemed as "illiterates from disuse." The books used in this course were the ones that I had received in my CARE kit, thanks to the folks back home. It was my hope that I could channel the readings and ideas in the books into actual health projects. The course included booklets with titles such as "Pure Water," "Care of Milk," "The Rural House," and my pet project, "Latrines, Their Construction and Use." If enough people were interested and willing to take the course, this could be a way to improve their own lot and create some enthusiasm for doing more.

I came back to La Toma all excited about the prospects and

spent a couple of days typing up stencils (in order to make multiple copies) for the booklet "The Danger of Flies." Pretty exciting stuff, eh? However, so much disease was transmitted by them in this environment where the pigs, fowl and their fecal material were everywhere, and there was very little refrigeration. I ran the stencils off on Padre Arias' mimeograph machine, hoping to use them when we went out to encourage people to attend and to conduct interviews to determine their interest and willingness. In order to schedule our visits, I took the results over to the school director, who was to head up the literacy project here. This was the first week in October, and she didn't think we should start it until after the Virgin of El Cisne (remember her?) was carried from Loja and back to El Cisne on November 1st. A <u>one-month</u> delay at minimum, and maybe she didn't want to bother with it at all. The air pretty much went out of my balloon with that news, and I occupied myself with my own version of the "battle against flies" that I could use as a showcase model.

One item in the CARE booklet that caught my eye was an evaporation type cooler, a sort of iceless "ice-box." It consisted of a wooden frame about the size of a five-foot high by one-and-on-half foot square display case. The wood is covered first with screening and placed in a pan of water. The unit is then covered with burlap, the bottom of which sits in the water, and through capillary action draws the water up, and the food inside on shelves is kept cool through evaporation. This keeps it free from flies, crawling insects, roaches and other multilegged "varmits," as Yosemite Sam would say.

I got all the materials together and built the thing in about a week, proudly displaying it outside my room with some food in it. With all the materials, the unit was probably pretty pricey for a lot of the families in town, but I wrote up a budget for the materials listed in terms of equivalent costs for bottles of Puro

Lojano. I later donated it to the family downstairs when the enthusiasm I hoped would ensue never occurred. In retrospect, the smart thing would have been to take it down to the home economics type class at the girls' school. This was nothing like the Home Ec. classes being taught in the U. S. at the time, as it had very little to do with stoves, ovens, or anything electric. It really was about sewing, household management, and the open fire cooking done in most homes.

The other effort I was making at the time was to help a couple of talented individuals find decent correspondence courses. One was a father of seven children, who needed to find a good course on diesel engines. He had worked at the sugar mill for seventeen years and had familiarity but wanted to show that he had some certification, and that piece of paper could improve his lot. I asked for some help from my father who was a teacher and counselor of foreign students at the Milwaukee Vocational School, and we were able to guide him to a reputable provider. There were too many others selling courses that provided worthless certificates that were not recognized by anybody.

On the library front, the inquiry to my mother about finding a sponsor had backfired. She mentioned it to some of the faculty, and they got the impression that I was looking to hit on the students for contributions for this effort. As I mentioned, our little school (I was in a graduating class of 72) had produced about six or seven Volunteers within two years. One of the teachers pointed out that they didn't want to play favorites. I was informed of their reaction and made it clear through my mother that was not my intent. I explained that what I was thinking about was more of a "People to People" type project, where a civic organization such as the Kiwanis Club or Women's Club were known to help with these sorts of things. I hadn't intended to petition the school, and this was particularly delicate as it could have looked like they would be playing favorites, especially since my mother was a teacher and my father on the school board. It was bad press, but I hoped my response cleared it up. At least the school was again going to be sending a CARE contribution, for which I was very grateful.

I still hoped to avoid the appearance of the *patron* passing out goodies, which was the *modus operandi* of most of the local politicians, so whatever I did with this year's funds would be presented as a "Gift from the People of the United States." And unless I saw a little more enthusiasm for the library project from other than Luis, I wasn't going to get too excited. One of the booklets in the CARE package was called, "Creating a Village Library." I would be prepared if and when they were ready.

FINISHING TOUCHES AND A BUMPY START

THIS PERIOD WAS REALLY GETTING ME DOWN. THE LA TOMA school was about finished. My great plans for projects were dead or on hold. Gonzanamá was off to a very slow start. My gang was gone. For better or worse, John Smith was gone and even Doc Caplin had been replaced. In an effort to cheer myself up, I looked at the option of moving into a well-lit room that had been vacated by the foreman of the Guarderas' operation but discovered it was twice the cost of what I had now, so I dropped that idea.

Since there were four families around the courtyard, my every coming and going was a matter of common knowledge. One day Marlene had the temerity to come down to my room (with the door open of course) to look at a book on the United States that interested her. Rumors that we were *enamoradas,* in love, made the rounds after that visit. My custom of sitting in front of her mother's store with her while we played Chinese Checkers for the whole world to see, probably contributed to the rumor mill as well. Those visits served two purposes. The first was that I avoided the "invitations" for *trago* fests, and the second was that she was a very nice, well informed, good looking young woman with whom I could have an intelligent conversation. I have no doubt that over time she came to have designs on me, and under different circumstances I might have envisioned us together. However, life in La Toma, post Peace Corps with Marlene? Doing what? Paid by whom for what? I knew in my head it would not be anything that would come to fruition. My future plans had been pretty much set in place. I was reminded of that when both Ann and my parents sent me clippings of engagement announcements that had appeared in their respective local papers.

My career plans included graduate school and hopes of entering the Foreign Service. In my spare time I started sending out feelers to a number of universities, seeking information on scholarships and getting applications sent down to me. Graduate schools that had good reputations for political science and international relations included Penn State, Georgetown, North Carolina and my alma mater Wisconsin. I had gotten wind that we could take the Graduate Record Exams down here. After a number of the usual screw ups and delays in sending and receiving mail, I was finally able to properly register for them. But these were things that seemed far down the road as I dealt with what was left of the day-to-day details of finishing the La Toma school. And there were a lot of them.

From the outside the school appeared finished. *Maestro* Illescas put the finishing touches on his work and was ready to head down to another town to make sure another school there was ready for its inauguration. Inside there were still two rooms that needed ceilings and dividers to be built and installed. We needed a little more paint here and there and a limited number of electrical connections completed. The pipes for the plumbing and sewers had arrived, and the *maestro* agreed to put them in before he left for good. John Mulligan came out, and he and I did the surveying for the location for the pipes. The excavation and installation of them would entail about three or four weeks of work.

One night we borrowed a tractor from the sugar mill. With one last "*minga*" we leveled the area between the two classroom buildings, and with the help of lanterns and a little "*trago* power," we finished at 11:30. This effort made it easier to ask for and build a basketball court. That night we learned the committee had decided the date for the inauguration would be November 18th. We had to get everything in place by then.

I spent the next days (I lost count) running in and out of Loja to make sure people were getting paid, attending to paperwork and getting the final eight gallons of varnish for the ceilings and doors. It was the typical hassle. I needed the approval from Ruilloba, and he was nowhere to be found. The committee had decided that they wanted a chain link fence around the school. Luis Garcia and I went to see the mayor about that and got approval for a load of fence pipes for the project. It was left to me to handle the logistics problem of getting them from the Municipality's yard down to the area where the "*mixtos*" were gathered and allowed to park. I tried to convince a *mixto* driver to come down the fifteen blocks and pick them up, but without success. "Too big a drive," he said. I looked again for Ruilloba to get the approval for the varnish and see if he could get Joe Kelly to take the fence pipes out in the Peace Corps Jeep. Time was of the essence because I hoped to put the varnish load on a truck, and the store was going to close. At about 4:00 I finally found Ruilloba but not Kelly. I got the approval signed, ran to the store, got the varnish and lugged it down to the *mixto* station just in time to see the truck turning the corner and heading for La Toma. I stayed in Loja that night.

The next day I tried again and got the fence posts down to the station at 9:50, missing another *mixto* by about two minutes. I was finally able to tell my sad tale of woe to a sympathetic driver who agreed to take both the fence posts and the varnish out for free. They went out on the bus at 12:00. I had done my part, and now the finishing touches were up to the painters.

Later, I had to make one final run into Loja to get a load of plywood that would be used for folding doors to create dividers in every other room. While I was there, I ran into the school inspector from Gonzanamá. He asked me, in so many words, "Where the hell have you been?" Of course, Ecuadorians are much too polite to say it that bluntly, but that was the essence of it. He said he had had a room ready for me for the last fifteen days, and everybody was waiting to meet me. I told him I had been very busy, but I would try to get down there that week.

I was good to my word. I went down there two days later and discovered that whatever room he claimed they had for me was not ready. I stayed in a *pension* that night where the only available facilities were a block and a half away. The next day I accompanied our contracted driver to see how much gas he was using driving from Gonzanamá to Cariamanga to obtain the sand they needed. The bills he had been submitting seemed a little suspicious. I discovered it only took twenty gallons instead of the thirty he had been charging us. The other ten gallons had been used up in his local hauling business in and around Gonzanamá and charged to our account. To make up for it, I told him we would only be paying for ten gallons until the account was even. Justo came through Cariamanga while I was there, and thankfully, I was able to get a ride back to Gonzanamá with him to avoid an unpleasant ride back with the driver. We met for an hour or so with the committee there and then headed back to La Toma.

Some good things were still happening. I told my good friend Ruben Patiño that Sunday marked one year for me in Ecuador, so we planned on going down to another friend's orchard to cook up some corn on the cob to celebrate the occasion. Ruben had heard from Juvenal Galarga of the Guarderas group that it was also my birthday, so they gave me a semi-surprise party. They invited all the male members of the English class, and we had a chicken dinner and numerous toasts on my behalf. I told them how much I appreciated their effort, kindness and friendship. It was rewarding to have a genuine, spontaneous occasion, and it gave me some sense that I had made some kind of positive impact.

More evidence of some good things happening was that the Centro Cultural had a meeting and decided to start a savings and credit cooperative. I had passed out the information on these four months prior, one to Suco, one to Padre Arias and another to Luis Garcia. I had pushed and pursued the idea for about a month and then figured it was going the way of all the others I had been championing. Now here it was, proof again, that all things come to him who waits. (Not always, but if he pushes hard enough while he waits....)

A new co-op Volunteer had arrived in Loja, and I made arrangements to have him come out and give whatever assistance he could provide. In these small towns, cooperatives were probably the best answer to economic progress. To top things off I had a talk with Padre Arias about the water well situation. He was still in favor of completing that project and, if the good Padre was for it, in this town you can be sure it was going to happen.

I made my promised trips to Gonzonamá, and I had to be there on Thursdays and Fridays to sign for the gasoline supply that was used for the truck transport. While I was there, I pushed the committee to get their people out to get enough supplies on hand to start the project. The *maestro* and I agreed that we would like to finish this school in seven months, so as to have it finished before I left the country - a noble goal but, given the start, a challenging one. I had my doubts. The room they had promised still hadn't materialized, and I stayed in a flea bag room above one of the stores in town. In riding with the truck driver and working in the rain while doing so, I managed to come down with another nasty cold, which wasn't helping my view of Gonzanamá or anything else.

CELEBRATE!

My cold was really getting to me, and I went into Loja and "got shot," twice for hepatitis and once for bubonic plague, though I felt like I already had both. In spite of that feeling, I wasn't going to miss the opportunity for a good dinner at the hotel. The Loja Hotel was now under new management, and there was finally a place in Loja where you could get a steak, and that's exactly what I had.

I had to return to La Toma on Saturday, as there was a dance at the basketball court that night to raise money for the school inauguration. That afternoon Ruben came over with a bucket of spray to fumigate my room with something designed to kill bedbugs, termites, and all sorts of other crawling things that seemed to be attacking me in the night. I don't know if they had anything to do with my feeling lousy but I was grateful for the help.

There was an intense competition before the dance started. Numerous booths were set up around the basketball court to see who could raise the most money: bingo, other games of chance, competitive games, and the like. The teachers from the girls' school and the Centro Cultural had bingo, but the Centro Cultural touted their games with a loudspeaker, doing very little to improve their public relations with the school teachers as the night went on. They kept at it so intensely that the dance did not start until 10:30. I stayed for a little while, but not even *trago* could perk me up so I headed for home and to bed.

My cold and maybe the reaction to the doctor's shots really hit me on Sunday, and I spent most of it in bed, totally missing the big arrival of the Virgin of El Cisne. She remained in the church all week, and then on Friday she was "processed" down to the next town of San Pedro, and on to El Cisne. Now I had missed her twice. The way they talked about "*Mamita Virgin*" and "*La Reina,*" the Queen, boggled my Protestant mind at the time. I thought about mentioning, "It's just a statue," but I feared being taken for a heretic and burned at the stake. I would not really say it out loud, of course, but the veneration was incredible. I spent two more days recuperating and finally returned to the world on Wednesday.

I learned that the floors for the school latrines would arrive as soon as the "good lady" left town. I also heard that Lyndon Johnson was re-elected in a landslide over Goldwater. In a letter home, I pondered whether it was not so much a vote for Johnson as it was a rejection of Goldwater. Most historians agree that Goldwater's campaign marked the start of a long trend of political and racial division in our country.

On the Gonzonamá front, I found out they had managed to get thirty-five truckloads of rock assembled but only fifteen truckloads of sand, which is about half of what had been agreed upon. I decided not to head down there for a bit because the truck we had been using was now being used on another site, and there was little to be gained by my presence. And, we had a celebration to plan here in La Toma.

I spent the week before the inauguration in a frantic rush back and forth to Loja to get the final bits of plumbing and electrical items, and a specialty paint for built-in blackboards. They were a "first" for the school and much better than the flimsy, free-standing things that had been used in the classrooms. New desks and benches for all the rooms had been donated, and we put them in place the night before the big day. We also swept, cleaned and polished, and were ready for the arrival of the "big cheeses."

They arrived on Wednesday, November 18th, and "big" they were! The entourage included two members of the ruling *junta*, the heads of the Agency for International Development in Ecuador, all of the *jefes* (bosses) from the Ministry of Education, and those involved in the School Construction Program as well: Watson, Justo and the rest. It all went off like clockwork – and not the usual Ecuadorian "clockwork"! The kids were once again in their Sunday best all lined up in a row on both sides of the schoolyard through which the officials passed. The drum and bugle corps in their little blue campaign hats and blue coats did their thing. The school construction committee members and the faculty from all the schools in town were there. Flags waved and the usual number of patriotic speeches and accolades ensued. Watson even gave me a big *abrazo,* a hug, even though he couldn't remember my name. Celebrations were held in the classrooms with champagne flowing and not a few bottles of *trago* made the scene as well, and then the official entourage went on to their next event.

I took a number of pictures of the whole process: the parade, teachers, students, and the *Maestro* and his crew. I wanted to remember this day as it was the culmination of a lot of work and community effort, and I wanted a record of this one. I was scheduled to attend another in Vilcabamba the next day, the one the *maestro* had been called to finish up, but I had my fill of self-congratulatory oratory and took a pass. As I looked back on this ten-month effort, it was time to look ahead to an effort that was ten months away. I arranged to take the Graduate Record Exams, and they were being held in Guayaquil in two days.

Luis García (in black suit on the left) keeps an eye on the drum and bugle corps as they lead the Junta, Chiefs and other dignitaries to the school inauguration.

Maestro Illescas and I in front of the multi-colored new school building after the inauguration ceremonies.

LOOKING AHEAD

ARMOND JOYCE AND I FLEW DOWN TO GUAYAQUIL TOGETHER on Friday and spent most of the day talking with a number of other Volunteers who had come down for the same purpose. The big adventure of the day was hunting down four of our very own #2 pencils required for the GRE. I had ordered one of the Getting Ready for the GRE books, as well as some others to be better prepared, but they hadn't arrived on time to be of any use. So, we "prepared" by going to see the movie, *The Great Escape*, that night.

On Saturday morning we all marched over to the testing center with the normal concern for "being on time" that most Americans carry with them like an internal alarm clock. When we got there, the woman from the U. S. Consulate said they couldn't get the tests out of customs and we would have to take the test the following week. We had a big discussion about which day would best suit the assembled cast and decided on the following Saturday for the event. It was really amazing to watch the resignation and relative calm with which the group took the news. If this sort of thing happened, say, two months or so after we had arrived in the country, there would have been great indignation, amazement, anger and complaining. Now it was just a shrug of the shoulders and, "That's Ecuador."

Due to the lack of funds and the fact that we would have to

make this trip again the following Friday, Armond and I decided not to fly back to La Toma. We left on a river barge instead at 8:00 in the evening and headed south down the river that led into Guayaquil until we reached Puerto Bolivar at 3:00 a.m. In Puerto Bolivar, the port that serves the city of Machala and the south of Ecuador, we caught a bus at 4:00, and I arrived in La Toma at 12:30 Sunday afternoon. A trip that took approximately an hour in a DC-3 took sixteen and a half hours by land. This is just another example of the state of transportation conditions in 1964 Ecuador. It was primarily the bad roads, but the numerous military check points along the way did not help either.

Since the school was finished, I spent most of that week attempting to fill out applications for the schools I selected. I decided to apply to Wisconsin, Stanford, and Penn State. I had to shift gears mentally to get back in the world of academic thinking. I had been so far removed from all this administrivia for so long and the slow mails were not helping. Wisconsin had not as yet sent me my applications, and Penn State had sent only one of the two necessary forms. I needed transcripts for all these applications and sent off requests to have those forwarded and to request again that the Political Science Department send me applications. It also dawned on me that I hadn't done much to nurture my professors. I spent some time writing to old classmates to get the proper first and last names of some of them to see if they would be willing references if needed. And just to add to the confusion, I applied to take the Law School Admission Test (LSAT.) Since all of these required fees to be sent along, that week included a trip into Loja to cash my birthday checks and convert them into cashier's checks to accompany all the paperwork. On Friday, Armond and I boarded the plane once again for Guayaquil. "*Déjà vu* all over again."

I took the GRE exam and was painfully reminded that I had

not been using math for five years, other than totaling up the cost of bricks, cement, nails, lumber, and the like. And none of that helped. I spent the rest of the week up to my ears in books and papers studying for the Foreign Service Exam and trying to finish school and scholarship applications. It seemed that every time I thought I was done, another set of required forms would arrive in the mail. The Foreign Service Exam was scheduled to be given in Quito the following week. I planned to take that on a Saturday and then spend a couple of days there afterward. That made three weeks in a row that I had not been to Gonzanamá, but I was counting on their normal amount of dilly-dallying that would delay the start of construction until the middle of December.

UP IN THE AIR

I FLEW UP TO QUITO ON TAME (TRANSPORTES AEREA MILITAR del Ecuador) airlines. The route was La Toma to Guayquil to Quito. For the first leg of the trip, I was on one of the DC-3 cargo planes that hauled both cargo and passengers. Apparently, the process was cargo in to La Toma and people out. The plane only had jump seats, the kind that any red-blooded paratrooper would use, and that's where we sat on the flight into Guayaquil. It was a very disconcerting feeling, sitting sideways on the take-off and landing. The second leg of the trip from Guayaquil to Quito was in a new and more well-appointed DC-6 with standard passenger seating that more than made up for the flight from La Toma.

The Foreign Service Exam was a shock to the system, being multi-part and three hours long, but with welcomed ten-minute breaks every hour. In spite of my cramming, I discovered that in addition to my deficiencies in math, my exposure to art, literature and science left a lot of room for improvement. If I was to succeed with these standardized tests I would need to "brush up on my Shakespeare."

As it happened, I arrived in Quito on the weekend of the celebration of the city's founding. It was a wild scene with people wandering the streets, each one with his bottle of *trago* or the Quito version of P*uro* which is freely offered to whomever they encounter. Great shouts of "*Viva Quito*" and then it's down the hatch. There were bands on every other corner and dancing in the street with even the gringos doing the famous national dance, the *San Jaunito*, in fine fashion. The locals were impressed.

No flights were available on Monday, so on Tuesday I flew down to Guayaquil with Wally Benson, who had also taken the exam. That night we went to see *Fate Is the Hunter*, a movie about a plane crash which was an ominous prelude to the flight we would take back to La Toma the next day.

We took off in clear skies, but as we approached our destination, we entered a thick cloud bank. I noted that the clouds were almost as thick as the lenses of the glasses I had seen the pilot sporting as he entered the plane. I think it was the first time I had seen a pilot wearing glasses other than sun glasses. About forty-five minutes into the flight, we dropped air speed and circled about four times over the nearby town of Catacocha and, for a moment, it looked like we were going to head back to Guayaquil. Then suddenly the plane gained altitude, as if we were possibly avoiding a mountain and then, almost as quickly, dropped down again into the Catamayo Valley, as scenes from *Fate Is the Hunter* danced in my mind. The passengers grew more apprehensive as we circled La Toma five times through the fog before the pilot abruptly set the plane down, speeding along the runway and then coming to a sudden stop, the engines roaring. The emotionally drained but relieved passengers departed, thankful to be back on *terra firma* once again. Flying TAME into or out of La Toma was often a real adventure.

ENDINGS AND NEW BEGINNINGS

I CAME BACK TO LA TOMA WITH EVERY GOOD INTENTION OF heading down to Gonzanamá. Really. However, that "road to hell" that is "paved with good intentions" took me in a different direction. I went into Loja to get my extra cot and a sleeping bag to take along. While there, I received a telegram from Armond informing me that we had to go to Guayaquil the next morning for the Ford Fellowship interviews. I had only just applied in late November. He wasn't sure if the interviews were to be conducted in Guayaquil or in Quito. Either way we had to fly down to Guayaquil, which we did the next day. We then found out the interviewer was flying into Quito the next day so we flew up there early and met him at the airport.

The interview was an hour and a half long and was based on essay type questions to which I had responded and sent in earlier. The interviewer dutifully wrote down every word I said. I wondered if the guy ever heard of tape recorders or rapid note taking. (Apparently not.) As you might gather from what you're reading, I may be prone to a little wordiness. Here, even though I've made an attempt to cut and edit (and it may still not be enough), my apologies for that. However, it was a real challenge for someone of my personality type to be careful of every word that came from my mouth - because if it came out, down it went. After the interview, and still low on funds, Armond and I just hung out the rest of the day and made a return trip to La Toma the next day. However, chalk up one more week where I hadn't darkened the Gonzanamánian door.

When I got back to La Toma, I met with Engineer Ruilloba, who said he was going to send a work crew down to Gonzanamá the following week. It looked like they finally had enough materials on hand to begin digging trenches for the foundation. That was good news.

The other bit of absolutely great news was that the good Padre and the Centro had made the decision to turn that dust bowl of the central plaza (that I had described when I arrived) into a real park. I drew up what I thought would be a good design. Having had no experience in such things, it was pretty standard stuff: a central circle with a monument of some sort; arms radiating out to the four corners; benches; a perimeter walkway and some trees here and there. I gave it to Padre Arias. He, Suco, and a few other officials of the Centro Cultural decided they would make a trip to the Municipality of Loja to see if they could get financial assistance and help for the park project and an official blueprint for its design and construction.

The excitement around the park project was palpable. The Centro and the Padre had already generated enough enthusiasm and arranged for eight truckloads of stone to be brought into the plaza in order to get the park campaign underway.

The good news kept coming! Army Lieutenant Ochoa told me that he was going to have his men use the Cinva-Ram to make bricks for latrines. In addition, Padre Arias had decided he would personally teach the lessons on health and hygiene, so that was another "early Christmas present" I heard upon my return. Maybe the secret to getting things done was to get out of town.

As the year drew to a close, I was feeling like an old veteran. I had worked on the construction of two schools and both had

Soldiers try out the Cinva-Ram machine.

been inaugurated within the year; I taught English classes; planted a few seeds through the CARE publications regarding latrines, health issues, and libraries; a savings and loan co-op was to be formed; and I coached an enthusiastic, if not always winning, girls' basketball team. Now it was time to see what the new year would bring. But first, we needed to close out this one.

It was very tough to get into the Christmas mood in this hot tropical setting. I was running low on money due to all my travels to Guayaquil and Quito. I hadn't bought presents, and my letters begged forgiveness from the folks back home, promising them I would make up for it on my return. Thankfully, I received a couple of checks from home for Christmas but nothing that would fund a vacation. Since, by Peace Corps regulations, I was required to take a vacation, I was reduced to getting a little financial help from my friends. So, I got a loan from a delightful, fun-loving new Volunteer, Roger Rupee, who had arrived in October, and that paid for my airfare. I also hit up our new boss for some traveling funds. I had spent the last Christmas in Quito high in the Andes, and I had enough of mountain air for the time being. Instead, I headed for Playas, a nice little spot on the beaches of the Pacific. Rodger was also up for the trip.

We flew out of La Toma on the 24th, and the first thing I did when I got into Guayaquil was to make reservations for my Christmas call to Ann. I spent the evening going to a movie and sitting at one of the sidewalk restaurants with Roger and a couple of other Volunteers who were also heading for Playas. When it came time to make the call on Christmas Eve, as I had done the year before, the lines were jammed, and when I finally got through on Christmas day, the reception was not good. At $3.60 a minute it was hardly worth the effort, but it was the sum total of my Christmas "gift" that year. Remember this was the time and place where one could get a good steak dinner for $1.75. After completing the call, we went out to Playas and stayed at a nice old (but very clean) *pensión* called Meyers. It was right on the beach, and I spent a good part of Christmas day in and out of the Pacific Ocean. To top it off, the food at the place rivaled my top choice for the best meal in Ecuador.

After two days there, we packed fourteen people into a small station wagon and headed for another resort we heard about in Salinas, a beach resort town at the westernmost point in Ecuador. It was a mistake. The rooms were bad; the food was skimpy; and the hotel was four blocks from the beach. The grass was not greener, and we should have stayed at Meyers. After one night there we headed back to Guayaquil. On Wednesday we flew back up to La Toma, and I went directly into Loja to retrieve my last month's salary and my travel pay, which had finally arrived. I reimbursed my "financiers" and paid off the rent at the apartment, cutting my available funds by half in a matter of hours.

The rent I paid was the last one for that place. The last of our apartment's roommates had married and taken off for the States. I spent most of Wednesday and Thursday moving my things and what was left of Wally Benson's stuff out of our old place and into the apartment that Roger Rupee had rented. The new line up was Roger, Wally, John Kostishack and me.

We had a New Year's party at the Peace Corps office in Loja, and quite a party it was. The office only occupied one or two rooms and the rest was Mike Aguirre's apartment, which was commonly referred to as "The Frat House" by the Loja Volunteers. There were a few locals there, but it was mostly a gringo party fueled by ample, tax-free Johnny Walker Red that Mike had acquired. There were a number of new Volunteers, strange faces to me, that had come in October along with Roger's group - engineers, co-op people and others I had not yet met. Mike Agurrie was heading up to Quito to meet the new school construction contingent, which would mean there would be even more that I wouldn't know. Mike said one of them would be sent to Gonzanamá. "The cavalry was coming!" Roger and I celebrated that fact far into the night, if not that fact, then some other fact. It didn't matter. 1965 had arrived!

...AND WHILE I WAS OUT

October, November and December, 1964

Politics:

- A protest launches the start of The Free Speech Movement as three thousand students at the University of California, Berkeley surround a police car to stop them from arresting a CORE student who refused to show his ID card.
- Police arrest 800 students involved in a massive sit-in at UC, Berkeley in support of The Free Speech Movement and in defiance of the Regent's decision to punish students for previous civil disobedience.
- While campaigning in New York City, President Johnson promises creation of "The Great Society."
- Goldwater declares that "forced integration is just as wrong as forced segregation."
- President Johnson says, "We are not about to send American boys nine to ten thousand miles away to do what Asian boys should be doing for themselves."
- Ronald Reagan tells of his decision to switch from Democrat to "another course." He complains of unfair taxes and asks whether a "little intellectual elite in a far-distant capitol can plan our lives for us better than we can ourselves," enhancing his reputation with Republicans.

- Lyndon Johnson defeats Barry Goldwater garnering over 60% of the popular vote. Goldwater takes only Arizona and five segregated southern states: Louisiana, Mississippi, Georgia, Alabama and South Carolina. Democrats take both the Senate and the House.

Civil Rights:

- Martin Luther King Jr. becomes the youngest person to receive the Nobel Peace Prize for his work in leading non-violent protests against racial discrimination in the U. S.
- FBI Director J. Edgar Hoover describes Martin Luther King Jr. as "the most notorious liar in the country" after King accuses FBI agents in Georgia of failing to act on complaints filed by blacks.
- The U. S. Supreme Court rules in Heart of Atlanta Motel v. U. S. based on the Civil Rights Act, that entities providing public accommodations cannot discriminate on racial grounds.

Vietnam:

- North Vietnamese forces launch pre-dawn mortar attack on Bien Hoa Airport killing four U. S. servicemen, wounding seventy-two and destroying five B-52 bombers.
- The U. S. National Security Members agree on and send a plan for a two-stage escalation of the bombing of North Vietnam to President Johnson which he and his top advisors agree to implement.

Space:

- The Soviet Union successfully launches a three-man spacecraft and returns it to earth after 24 hours.

- NASA successfully launches Mariner 4 probe headed to Mars to send back televised pictures in 1965.

International:

- The Russian Presidium votes to retire Premier Khrushchev and replace him with Alexei Kosygin.
- China explodes an atomic bomb.
- Belgian paratroopers liberate over 1,600 Europeans who had been taken hostage by a rebel army leader in the Democratic Republic of the Congo.
- Che Guevarra addresses the U. N. General Assembly, and a bazooka attack is launched at U. N. Headquarters as Cuban anti-communists demonstrate at the entrance.
- Stemming from the riots in January at the Panama Canal, the United States offers to negotiate a new treaty.

Culture:

- The film version of *My Fair Lady*, starring Audrey Hepburn, premiers in New York City.
- In the U. S. the Catholic Church changes its liturgy, including the use of English instead of Latin.
- The animated stop-motion feature *Rudolph the Red-Nosed Reindeer*, based on the song of the same name, premiers on NBC.
- Sam Cooke, African-American singer and song writer is shot and killed in Los Angles.

CHASING TWO RABBITS

AN OLD CONFUCIAN SAYING NOTES, "THE MAN WHO CHASES TWO rabbits, catches neither." My last six months in Ecuador were a good example of that. I had four rabbits in my sights, and each needed a concentration of effort which I was having a heck of a time juggling. The first was the continuing effort to make things happen in Gonzonamá; the second was to move the newly energized projects in La Toma. Three and four were in the "Look Homeward, Jerry" department. The third rabbit was to nail down acceptance at a grad school or law school and find scholarships to help make that happen. The fourth was my pending marriage now set for August 21st of 1965.

The grand plan (or "magical thinking" depending on your interpretation) was to go home, get married, attend grad and/or law school and get a job in the Foreign Service or another related area. I was still working to find references, and my old political science advisor Dr. Llewelyn Pfannkuchen, had suggested a number of other schools to which I should be applying. I hadn't heard from the University of Wisconsin which was my first natural choice from a financial standpoint. The Foreign Service Exam results came in, and I was three points under the cut off for passing. That year 7,000 people took the exam. 3,000 passed and the number of available positions was 140. Since both the GRE and the FSE study books had arrived after I had taken the tests, I determined to give the Foreign Service Exam one more shot. I added that onto my "Things to Do" list.

On the Gonzanamá front, the construction was progressing. I decided to do a four-day stint in Gonzanamá and then three days in La Toma. That was the plan, but the execution had not always been that successful. The arrival of the new Volunteer would have some effect on my schedule, depending on his background and comfort with the language and customs. The Gonzanamá workers were running short on materials because the local committee was short on money. We had to lay off a worker, and then Ruilloba borrowed the carpenter for a week. But the foundations for both units were still completed, and a *minga* to pour the base plate and columns on which the brickwork would be laid had been successful. I got a truck from the Provincial Municipality in Loja, and the *maestro* and I loaded up what few materials had been left over in La Toma. Our plan to finish this school in seven months was looking good for the moment. Mike Aguirre informed me that the new contingent of Volunteers included a guy named Paul Bond who was coming down to work in Gonzanmá on a permanent basis. However, he wanted me to continue there until Paul got properly settled in. Mike also wanted me to check on and help Tom Wegs, another new Volunteer assigned to San Pedro, the town about ten miles to the west of La Toma. La Toma would continue to be home base, and I would be heading out south and west from there. That was good news because there was still a lot to be done in La Toma.

Padre Arias was handling the health courses in a fine manner, and he was also folding in religious practices he thought would aid in that effort. He was happy with that mix, and who was I to differ? It was getting done. As I reached one year in La Toma, I met with Suco who filled me in on his and Padre Arias' commission to see the Loja mayor regarding the plans they had in mind.

I was pleased that the plans included many of the things that I had been trying to push ever since I arrived. The Municipality had promised to give the equivalent of $1,500 toward the park and would provide a grader to level the plaza where needed. In addition, as part of an urbanization project, they were going to use that grader to square off all the lots and streets. Most gratifying to me, they were taking over some vacant lots that owed back taxes and placing latrines on those. Suco also informed me that the Centro Cultural was going to change locations. At the new site, there would be a dedicated room for their library, and he consented to open it to the public. To top it all off, one of the "patrons" from the sugar mill family offered to provide funds for playground equipment to be placed in the park. La Toma would have latrines, a park with a playground, a library, and the Padre teaching health classes. A lot of this was still promises, but it was all a lot closer to realization than it had ever been, and I felt good about that.

In mid-January, I had gone into Loja to pick up some supplies and met with Engineer Ruilloba. There had been some lobbying for building a new girls' school. He told me maybe they could swing one or two rooms, but he didn't think they could do the whole thing. However, he hadn't counted on our wily Padre. When the Minister of Education and the heads of the Program came though the next Thursday after inaugurating a school in Macará, the committee hit them hard and came off with a promise to complete a new two-story building. The tricky old Padre had told the Minister that the rocks in the plaza had been collected for the school and that we "had sand in great quantities." We did, but it was all in the river. They started tearing down the old building the following week.

To move the proposed park along, I tried to get Jim Snyder to come out and help me measure off the dimensions of the park, but he was busy working with another new Volunteer on a huge new reservoir project down in San Pedro. I got John Mulligan to come out and help when he came out to work on the water project. Together we staked out the dimensions of the perimeter, which was the first thing to be laid.

Also, in the middle of the month, the new Volunteer, Paul Bond, arrived in Gonzanama and, not surprisingly, seemed to be a little nervous about the whole thing. He had a lot of trouble understanding people and almost as much trouble speaking the language. Paul was set up in a room there, which I hoped was better than the one I had. I decided to leave him on his own to get acclimated. A week and a half later, I was relieved to find that he seemed to be doing much better. Paul, 23 years old, hailed from Jonesborough, Arkansas, and had traveled extensively in the States. He knew his construction, having served a six-month stint in the Army with the Corps of Engineers, so I was reassured to hear that. Once he became at least a little more fluent in the language, I figured I could safely leave this one in his hands if I had to. I kept going down there to bring materials from Loja and make sure people were moving ahead. Paul seemed a little down in the dumps after a couple of weeks but cheered up a bit when we were able to change the living quarters he had initially been given.

In the midst of all these coming and goings, Ann sent me an initial list of wedding invitees. It listed thirty-five relatives, but only one of my friends, so I had some work to do to convince Ann and her mom to add more of my friends, especially those whose weddings I had attended. She had also sent down brochures of silverware, glasses and dishes to get my opinion on them. It was like seeing stuff from another world. The pictures featured sterling silver flatware, bone china and crystal stemware. I was happy if I had a fork and a plate that didn't have any amoebas on it! Clark Gable's famous line from *Gone with the Wind* came to mind, but I chose not to use it, discretion being "the better part of valor." She was also urging me to line up five groomsmen, something about which I hadn't given much thought. I knew I would ask my older brother, Tom, to be my best man, but I was not sure about the rest. One of my best friends from high school, Greg Schaefer, was still in the Peace Corps in Colombia and would not be available. Another, Wayne Wolfgram, was in the Army in Germany. Only Mel Heimark would be available, so it looked like I would have to count on the kindness of some of my fraternity brothers to help me out. I set out to track down a few of them who, it seemed, had gone to the four corners of the world. My next requirement was to show up and show up on time.

"AND OTHER DUTIES AS REQUIRED"

JANUARY ROLLED INTO FEBRUARY (AS IT ALWAYS DOES), AND MY concentration of effort was now on the park project, while still balancing the other things on my plate. (Those "other duties as required" as the job descriptions say.) On one of my runs into Loja for materials, I was shocked to see the place full of soldiers sporting rifles and submachine guns. It turned out that one of the leftist groups at the University of Loja had run a campaign for president of the student body. A Communist was elected, and the group had a big parade, which turned into a demonstration that had to be broken up by the military police. The guards I saw were there to make sure that no further outbursts took place. In spite of the fact that the *junta* had outlawed the Communist Party of Ecuador, there were still plenty of people involved who thought the only way the impoverished classes of the country would ever get any real attention was through communism. Even in La Toma, from time to time on my way to the school site, I would hear some wag taunt me with a growled "Vieeeeet naaaaagahm" as I walked along. Their numbers were few, but they were around and didn't think much of my presence.

When I came back from Loja, I found a couple of guys from the Municipality working on the alignment of the park dimensions again. Apparently, some of the *jefes* (bosses) in Loja wanted to change the plan a little. I had no problem with that, as I was far from being an architect. As long as the thing was built, I would be happy. We had a number of *mingas* to get the sand "we had on hand" from the river, and I found that my soft gringo feet needed a lot of TLC after that effort. Many of the *peones* wore crude sandals or no footwear at all, and their well-callused feet were impervious to the rocks and stones the river contained. Not so much for this guy.

I took a break in the middle of February to fly down to Guayaquil to take the Law School Acceptance Test. I had boned up on my math after the GREs just to be ready, but there was almost none at all on the LSAT. When I returned from taking the test, I went into Loja to see what plan for the park the Municipal boys had drawn up. I learned that they had prepared not one, but three options. A couple of days later they presented those options to Padre Arias and some other decision makers, and with their "go ahead" the final design was approved. It was official. We had ourselves an approved plan for the park.

While in Loja I also met with Engineer Ruilloba. He informed me that they would probably not start on the girls' school until May. Justo had to come down and sign the official agreement before the material collection could begin. "Probably just as well," I thought, because too many demands for *mingas* would start to overwhelm the community. That was the good news. The bad news for me was I was part of the School Construction Program and without that new school construction starting, I was finding myself with not a whole lot to do of an official nature. Paul Bond was in Gonzanamá, where I was still "in charge," but he was covering the necessary basics.

The calendar was helping me out a bit. It was *Carnaval* time again! And during *Carnaval* you may remember, nothing gets done. Officially, it did not start until the 28th of February but as usual, the troops had started the nonsense at least a week earlier.

One thing I was able to do was to present the Centro Cultural with some garden tools and a number of other items courtesy of the students of dear old Pewaukee High. They had sent a sizeable contribution, and I think I used it well. Unlike the previous year when I ordered from a catalogue and waited, this year I went directly to the CARE offices when I was in Guayaquil to take the LSAT. I selected two agricultural packages with tools for gardening; seven student education classroom kits; a classroom selection full of reams of paper, erasers, and pencils; and a bag of physical education gear. I also chose two village library kits, one for the Padre's school and the other for the Centro Cultural. In addition, I got two more sewing kits for my gang at the girls' school. I gathered all of these items, but when I went to the airport to depart for La Toma, I discovered I was twenty-seven pounds overweight. I was out of money and couldn't pay the fee. Fortunately, the airport attendant took pity on me, I think because they were CARE items, and let it go for free.

The gardening tools especially were a hit. I took time to attend one of the general session meetings of the Centro Cultural and made an official presentation of the gardening tools to them. I gave the other gardening tools to the boys' school, as they were going to start a CARE garden. (If they had a CARE garden, I figured they should have CARE tools.) The Centro wrote a big flowery note to my high school (in Spanish of course) thanking them profusely for their contributions.

Carnaval started on Sunday and went on with the usual shenanigans for almost a week. A few of the old Guarderas gang came out from Loja because, I guess, nobody does it better than La Toma. All that afternoon, we got sopping wet, powdered with flour and cornstarch and ended the day with a big dance. I managed to take photos of a few memorable scenes to send home after getting promised that no one would throw water at my camera. Monday was a double whammy with a party at Miguel Montaño's in the daytime. Then it was on to the Carrión hacienda (with all the cousins from La Toma and Loja), with the evening again ending in dancing fueled by the usual required libations. I had hoped without success it would all end on Tuesday, but it started up again at 9:00 a.m. and went well into the night, ending again with a dance, on which I, mercifully, took a pass.

I escaped to Loja on Wednesday and asked John Mulligan about a well drilling machine that the Municipality could make available. Unfortunately, it was being used elsewhere and would not be available for another month. I wasn't even sure I could get it out to La Toma, but it was one of the projects the Padre liked, and I had hoped to help make it happen. At that moment I had few other prospects. I made it back to La Toma the next day but not without being hit one too many times by flying water balloons when departing Loja.

In mid-March it was suddenly "all hands-on-deck" regarding the park project. It was nice to see some progress other than piles of sand and rock. I went into Loja to see a student engineer who was a good friend of Jim Snyder's and was becoming one of mine as well. Tom*á*s Vallejo was in charge of the Municipal Council's efforts for the park project and improving the layout and delineation of La Toma's streets. Broadly speaking, La Toma was being urbanized. It was the start of what would eventually turn La Toma into Catamayo.

Tomás said he was heading out to San Pedro to work on the reservoir project, but he would drop off the park plans with Padre Arias on the way. We planned to meet in San Pedro the next Sunday to help with the *minga* that Jim Snyder had put together. I went there with a carload of Volunteers as intended. When I saw Jim I asked if Tomás was there and he said, "No, he's working in La Toma." Wires crossed again! Since I was there, I pitched in for about an hour and a half and returned to La Toma.

Early on Monday I found Tomás already working on the streets and, after talking with the Padre and the committee members, we got the approval to stake out the plan that had been approved. Tomás and I worked on surveying and staking all day, but there was more left to do on Tuesday. However, during the day I had received a telegram from Paul in Gonzonamá telling me I should come down there with my radio. I thought he was either in trouble or there was some special broadcast he needed or wanted to hear. I caught a bus about 6:00 that evening and headed down there, only to find out he just missed listening to the radio. The crazy man figured since I had nothing to do, I ought to come down. I stayed that night, and we both caught the 5:30 a.m. bus back to La Toma on Tuesday morning. Paul justified his trip, as he had a wheel barrow tire that needed repair.

Tomás and I finished the job by Tuesday evening, staking out the entire park - the curves, the ellipses, and the walkways. The next day the Padre got a few students out of school and "Engineer Redfield" and Tomás Vallejo directed them in using pick axes and small shovels to dig trenches where we had placed the stakes that outlined the plan. This insured that even if it rained, or someone decided to pull up some stakes, we would still have the outline intact. The President of the Municipal Council, Tomás' ultimate boss, stopped by and promised two trucks to haul materials for the upcoming weekend's *mingas*. Armond was in town as well because his truck broke down. He and his young Ecuadorian helper stayed with me that night as Paul had done the night before. I was always glad to have English speaking guests, and Paul really liked the La Toma vibes. As additional good news, Armond promised me that he and Bill White were going to donate a number of trees and plants to the park project from the nurseries Bill managed for the Municipality. Bill would contribute and Armond, an arborist by training, would help plant them.

The pace slowed a bit after that busy week, but there was some progress on a lot of fronts. The *mingas* were going well on the weekends. Only one truck had showed up rather than the two that had been promised, but we made the best of what we had, getting eleven loads of sand and six loads of gravel delivered to the park site over the two days. The really good news was that the following weekend the members of the Centro Cultural were going to pitch in as well. I would like to think it was the fact that they had seen so many Volunteers busting their humps, they may have felt a little guilty about not pitching in and just leaving the work to folks from the poor side of town. The reality probably was, as with any civic organization, it was always good to be seen "doing the work."

I had been making my required trips down to Gonzanamá to see how things were progressing and found them to be doing well but short of bricks. They never did use the cement blocks they had planned to use. Fortunately, the Provincial Council had sent their truck back out, and we were able to use it for two weeks and build up a big inventory. The brickwork on about half the school was finished. Paul seemed to be much more settled, if not particularly ecstatic to be there. He had been talked into providing English classes as well and now had three of them going. He remarked to me, "Gee, this English business can really get away from you, can't it?" It surely can and it certainly had for me.

However, back in La Toma, my news in the English department was that we had finished the book! We had a little celebration following the last classes, and a number of students were asking for more. I didn't want to start what I couldn't finish and declined. I did, however, continue with Miguel Montaño and Ruben Patiño on an informal basis. They could accommodate my irregular schedule and were grateful for the chance. And I was glad to work with my now two best friends.

On a less happy note, I received my grades back from the Law School Admissions Test, and they were "nothing to write home about." So, I didn't. No, I really did, but that was the sum total of my report. If I wanted to get into any "good" law schools I would have to take it again. It looked like my option now was definitely grad school somewhere, but I had yet to hear from the University of Wisconsin or the University of North Carolina. Perhaps I should have taken a clue from the letter Professor Pfannkuchen had sent me recommending I apply to the University of New Mexico and a few other schools. Then maybe I would not have been so disappointed when I received a rejection letter from my dear old alma mater. My grade point average missed their cut off point by two tenths of a point and I was really disappointed. I let Ann know. She was devastated as she had envisioned renewing acquaintances and old haunts, as had I. As insurance, I sent off an official application with the required fees to Penn State, the other university from whom I had heard. It wasn't my first choice, but not having heard from anyone else at this point, I figured I better nail down one option just to be safe. But could we be happy in Happy Valley?

The future still looked murky except for one thing: I was going to get married. At least I received a response from one guy, Lowell Woodward, who was also a Volunteer. (He got Costa Rica.) He said he would be available to be a groomsman. That was two.

...AND WHILE I WAS OUT

January, February and March, 1965

Politics:

- The Free Speech Movement is victorious as a new chancellor is installed at the University of California, Berkeley and students are allowed to make speeches and protest from the steps of campus buildings.
- In his State of the Union address, President Johnson proclaims his Great Society and his plans to promote birth control abroad.
- President Johnson is inaugurated for his second term.

Civil Rights:

- Martin Luther King Jr. begins a drive to register voters in the deep South.
- As a result of the Civil Rights Act, a federal grand jury indicts 18 men for violating the rights of the three civil rights workers murdered in Mississippi in 1964.
- Malcom X is assassinated in front of 400 people. Assassins are described as members of Elijah Muhammad's Nation of Islam.
- On March 7th, what becomes known as "Bloody Sunday," some 200 Alabama State Troopers clash with 525 civil rights

marchers (including John Lewis) in Selma, Alabama, using clubs, dogs and tear gas. The event is broadcast on television bringing home the impact of the brutality.

- Martin Luther King Jr. leads a second attempt at a march from Selma, Alabama, to Montgomery and is stopped. James Reeb, a Unitarian Universalist minister, is beaten by white supremacists, goes into a coma, and dies two days later in a Birmingham hospital.
- Demonstrations all across the U. S. (including Michigan Governor, George Romney, leading 10,000 marchers) protest events in Alabama.
- Police in Montgomery clash with 600 members of the Student Nonviolent Coordinating Committee (SNCC.)
- In response to the events in Selma and Montgomery, President Johnson sends a bill to Congress that will form the basis for The Voting Rights Act of 1965. It is eventually passed and signed into law.
- Martin Luther King Jr. successfully leads a march of 3,200 civil rights activists from Selma to the capitol in Montgomery, Alabama.
- Civil Rights activist, Viola Liuzzo of Michigan, is shot and killed by four Klansmen as she drives activists back from Montgomery to their homes in Selma.
- *The Negro Family, The Case for National Action,* a controversial report from Patrick Moynihan, is published. It maintains that African-American poverty is more the result of the breakdown of the African-American family and the rise of single-family mothers than it is from economic conditions. The report is accused of racial bias and attacked by both the Left and the Right over the years.

Vietnam:

- President Johnson announces plans for increased bombing of North Vietnam.
- 3,500 U. S. Marines, the first combat troops, arrive in South Vietnam.
- The first teach-in against the Vietnam War is held at the University of Michigan.

Space:

- An unmanned Gemini 2 is launched to test numerous systems in space.
- Ranger 8 crashes into the moon after successfully photographing landing sites for Apollo program astronauts.

Culture:

- A new, live, color production of Roger and Hammerstein's *Cinderella* is shown on CBS.
- The movie version of the *Sound of Music,* starring Julie Andrews, premiers in New York City.

"Quo Vadis?" Once Again

An official park committee had now been constituted and, in spite of my previous involvement, I was not invited to be a member. I could have told myself that this was great progress, that the group was operating without my wise counsel, but the reality was something else. I suspected it was because I had gotten into a heated argument with the Padre, and he didn't want me on it. He told me as much afterward. We differed on how the park should be enclosed, and I think he thought that if I was on the committee, I would be pushing my opinion. He wanted a full fence all the way around the park, and I thought that would make it look restrictive. Again, in looking back, unless they corralled all those wandering pigs and dogs and fowl, he had a point. I was looking only at aesthetics. Frankly, I really didn't care as long as they got construction underway. I had my hopes dashed there as well. They decided not to start until two thirds of the way through April. This was Lent and April 18th was Easter Sunday. Then they could start.

My friend Ruben was on the committee, and I figured if I needed agenda pushed, he would be willing to be my advocate, if he agreed of course. In the meantime, I occupied myself with runs into Loja to talk with Tomás Vallejo, Armond Joyce, and Bill White about trees and required supplies. Tomás was just starting to draw up the plans for the materials, but he had already decided to line each walkway with a different species of tree so that the view from above would be one of colored lines and half circles. Armond and Bill provided me with a list of the different trees we could get from the Municipal nursery, and I passed that on to Ruben to present to the committee. I also found out that we would have three trucks available for the upcoming *mingas* that were planned. Regarding those *mingas,* I also discovered that the Provincial Council offered to pitch in 500 sacks of cement and the Municipal Council offered to pay for the mason and provide items from the Food for Peace Program. The meals would be used to feed the folks doing the *mingas* and for the *peones* doing the daily work once it got underway. Our school *mingas* were always supported by a group of women that served food and beverages to keep the workers happy. It was a picnic-like atmosphere when the work was finished. The town folks felt as if they were doing their part to help their kids, and indeed they were. The park project would be no different.

When I wasn't running into Loja, I was going down to Gonzanamá to check on the school there. I found that things were going along quite well and that Paul, now unofficially "Pablo," had things fairly well under control, but he still acted as nervous "as a long-tailed cat in a room full of rocking chairs." The work for the school started to ebb and flow with the rains, as we experienced a delayed winter. Rain hit harder in the higher altitude of Gonzanamá than it did in La Toma. But we still had our share.

In order to get the big *minga* day off to a good start, I missed an Easter dinner at Mike Aguirre's. Padre Arias was so busy blessing people, animals, birds, etc. that he had failed to call anyone with his standard loudspeaker announcement. As a result, only a small group was available to start digging out the trenches for the foundations. Our *minga,* consisting of only twelve people, lasted about fifteen minutes before it started to rain like crazy. With the small turnout and the rain pouring down, everybody was pretty demoralized. After waiting about an hour for the rain to stop, they drifted away one by one. I talked Suco into going with me to talk with the Padre, who by this time had about finished sprinkling Holy Water on the animals in the middle of the rainstorm. After we intervened, the Padre made his announcement, and the people came in numbers large enough to allow us to finish the full perimeter of the park in about two hours. At that point all that we needed was one of the engineers from the Municipality to provide some details and pointers on what the height of the foundations should be, and we would be underway.

About a week later, I was typing away on one of my many missives home when someone told me that the grader from the Municipality was in the plaza. I thought, "Good, they've arrived at last," and went out to meet them to give them some guidance. What I found was that the guy was already well underway levelling the area and had dug up or knocked over all the stakes that Tomás and I had put in. He said he was told to level the area. I was furious. We would have to redo the whole damned thing.

The day Tomás was to return, it dawned on me we would need a transit level to properly stake out the park, yet again, at the right elevations. I jumped on a 6:30 a.m. bus into Loja to remind him to bring it out, figuring I could return with him. As it so often goes in Ecuador, we passed each other, he on the way out and I on the way in. So, I jumped on the next bus back to La Toma where they were waiting for me. He hadn't brought it. We tried to wing it, using the leveling instrument we did have but to no avail. The Municipality sent the transit out the next day, and we spent all day Saturday and a half day on Sunday redoing our original effort at staking out and leveling the park.

A couple of days went by, and Tomás sent out the final plans for the park. After haggling with the mason over how much he was to be paid, which was substantial, we got the project started. After looking at the plans, we discovered there were a couple of areas that still needed addressing. One was where we dug foundations too low and another area that still needed to be completed. We again got the good services of about fifteen school kids, and finished the project. It got underway exactly ten days after it was supposed to start. In 1965 Ecuador, that was warp speed.

On one of my many trips into Loja, I had the chance to finally meet with Justo regarding the start of construction on the girls' school. They decided to go ahead with it and signed the contract, but it would not start until May 17th. That would be somebody else's baby. I invited Tom Wegs, the other new Volunteer whom I was "keeping an eye on" in San Pedro, to come up for the formation of the girls' school construction committee as he would be the one most likely to supervise this effort. We spent most of the day together since we had been told the meeting was supposed to be in the morning but was shifted to the evening. The committee decided that the new school would be built on the same site as the old. One half will be torn down, construction started and when completed, the girls would move in and the other torn down. I was not too impressed with the enthusiasm of this new committee but that would be Tom's problem, not mine. The torch had been passed.

In the highs and lows of my own future plans, I had one ray of hope. The University of North Carolina answered me and informed me that their departments had not as yet considered all the applications due to the volume they received that year. They said they would let me know within a couple of weeks. That, at least, was not a "no." What <u>was</u> a "no" was a notification I finally received from the Ford Foundation Fellowship. They "were happy to have considered me as a candidate, however...." Adding a little insult to injury was the fact that Armond, my apartment roommate, had received a Fellowship. He received a full ride to Penn State which included fees and tuition plus $1,800 for expenses (approximately $14,600 today.) Armond diplomatically pointed out that he was in forestry and there was probably a lot less competition there. That was kind, but Armond was very sharp, and his scholarship was well deserved. I was happy for him, but still wondered where my next dime was coming from.

As a last-ditch effort, I wrote an appeal letter to the University of Wisconsin asking them to reconsider my application and telling them of "*mein kampf*" (my struggles) - a humble Wisconsin boy who had worked my way through as a kitchen helper, waiter, laundry collector as well as serving three years in time consuming extracurricular activities with the YMCA and on the Wisconsin Badger yearbook, etc., etc. I knew it was a long shot, as there were plenty of folks with lots of extracurricular activities that had grades much better than mine. But it was worth a shot, as the U. W. was really where I wanted to be.

Tomás Vallejo and I prepare for construction of the park. In the background is the school where I taught my English classes.

Miguel Montaño, Suco's son and Suco Candela at a minga, digging the perimeter for the park.

PROGRESS, PACKING AND PARTYING

THE LAST COUPLE OF MONTHS IN LA TOMA WERE A MIX OF PUSHing for progress on the park; packing and shipping footlockers and duffel bags; "*despedidas*" (goodbyes); and farewell parties. It was time to wind down, turn over, muster-out and head home. In truth, I was very sad to do so.

The park project moved along, and by the end of May we had the foundations of the perimeter laid and topped with only a fifteen-inch wall. The much debated (by me) wall turned out to be just a fifteen-inch-high base, into which would go a wire chain-link that would not be blocking anything visually and, in turn, would keep all sorts of animals from foraging on the newly planted trees and shrubs. So, the good Padre was right. What was not clear to me earlier, was that there would also be a sidewalk outside the fence on which the good citizens of La Toma would one day do their *paseo,* the traditional leisurely evening stroll following dinner. By the time of my departure, trees and bushes had been designated but not yet been planted. We did manage to get the foundations for the inner walkways done before it came time for me to leave. You could at least tell there was a park about to be born.

By the second week of June, we had not completed as much on the park as I anticipated, in spite of the fact I had been working as much as possible to make it happen. People wondered why we didn't just hire some *peones* to finish the job. The reality was there wasn't enough money to pay them and they had me for free!

I invited Tom Wegs to come up from San Pedro to go over the park plans with him as he most probably would be involved if there was to be continuing involvement from the Peace Corps. He had to come up for another matter as well. The contract for the girls' school was finally about to be signed. Originally the Minister of Education was going to be involved in the signing, but he was prevented from attending by labor unrest in Guayaquil. Apparently, the populace was less and less happy with the *junta's* lack of reforms, and in Guayaquil they were letting them know. (By July there would be rioting in the streets that would have to be put down by the military police.) Tom was there for the more modest signing event, and the deal was sealed.

The middle of June also brought three pieces of good news. The University of North Carolina at Chapel Hill had accepted my application. More importantly, the University of Wisconsin's Political Science Department had decided to accept my appeal, and I gladly sent them my application. So, that part of my future was clear. I would be in the Masters' Program for Public Administration at the University of Wisconsin in Madison. The other bit of positive news came from Mike Aguirre. He told me he had submitted my name as a possibility for future Peace Corps work. There were four divisions: Recruiting, Training, Washington Staff, and Peace Corps Representative. He told me he had suggested other individuals for specific positions, but that I was the only one that he felt could be capable of handling any one of the four. This bit of positive reinforcement was rewarding and having a possible fallback position if the rest did not work out was a comforting thought.

That same week I had one day's notice that all my big luggage items had to be shipped from Loja to Quito by the 11th of June.

I quickly packed up everything I could (including books) into a footlocker and a duffel bag and went into Loja to send them off. The story was that all of these items would be shipped by air to our homes as of June 30th. I hoped so but had my doubts. That was putting a lot of trust in the mails. I had put a number of things up for sale such as my boots, my recorder and even my typewriter but had no takers, so I would be hauling them up to Quito if they were not sold by the time I left. I had been giving things away prior to this, mostly to Ruben and Miguel Montaño, so the "cupboard" was pretty bare by the end of June.

On June 5th we had a big farewell party in Loja for the Volunteers from the Heifer Project who were wrapping up just before our group. It was designated for them, however, as with so many of the School Construction gang in attendance, it was for us as well. The Loja paper, *Opinion del Sur,* printed an entry listing and thanking all the departing Volunteers who had served in the Province of Loja. The next day we had another *despedida* (farewell party) in San Pedro for all the gang that had worked in and around there. It included Mary Ann Mobley, a health worker from Oregon; Bill White, who had worked in the Municipality's nursery; and Jim Snyder who had completed the reservoir project there. People wanted to know when I was coming back. I hemmed and hawed about needing to continue my studies but hoped I could return in some manner. I didn't want it to end but <u>did</u> want it to end, just to be done with all the uncertainty. I didn't want to say, "I'll never see you again." In La Toma there were a number of individual and group goodbye parties, plus an official one from the Centro Cultural with many speeches in my honor; an inscribed aluminum dish (suitable for travel); an honorary membership medallion; and lots and lots of *trago*. There was a great deal of pressure on me to stay until the park was finished, but that would have entailed an extension, and I had some "other duties as required" to take care of on the other end. I had to be home to get married to the woman I had not seen for over ten months. There were a number of individuals in some areas who did extend for three months to get projects completed, but I was not to be one of them. If circumstances were otherwise, I may have done so. In fact, in Latin America the Peace Corps had come up with a new system. Starting in December of 1965, all Latin American tours of duty would be for twenty-seven months, with three months of training and a full two years in country. With four more months I might have been able to pull off the water project with a "We need water for the park angle." I told them, "I do not say, 'Goodbye to you, but rather, *hasta luego*', until we meet again." But it was not to be. I was through.

It was very difficult saying goodbye to the many fine people I had come to know including Ruben, Miguel, Suco, Padre Arias, the Carrións, the Garcías, the Bermeo family and Marlene in

Carlos Carrión, another teacher, and Marlene Bermeo with me at one of the school's graduation ceremonies.

particular. Marlene had been my confidant, my friend, had become my cheerleader, and, at times, goad. During my time in La Toma she was my dance partner at many holiday parties where she would make a point of being by my side. Admittedly, I didn't hesitate about returning the affection. We were very close friends by the end of my stay, and by this time I knew she was very sweet on me. But since I would not, or could not return that feeling in a way she had wished, she had become defensive, accusing me of not wanting her because she was "too much of color" or too dark. In other words, I would not have her because of racial bias. That, of course, was so much nonsense. Besides, I thought I had made it pretty clear to her that I was already taken.

I had made my commitment to Ann almost a year earlier and her letters kept me aware of it. For, while I was out, Ann had been planning all the details of our wedding: the bridal registries, the church, the music, the flowers, the reception details, and the honeymoon. The date was set. While I had been working on projects and becoming more and more entangled in the daily life of the people and the town where I had been working, Ann had been fully engaged in planning for the event she had been anticipating for over a year. My actual presence was needed to complete the scenario.

And now with all those goodbyes behind me, it was time to head up to Quito and "muster out," which I did on the last few days of June. It had been quite a journey. Looking back on all I had been through, the scoreboard read: two schools completed and one underway; a park in progress; a savings and loan co-op; a nascent library; health courses being run; and the promise of latrines to be built. There was still more that could have been done: the water project for upper La Toma, a basketball court for the school and much more. But those would be left for other days and other people. It was time to wrap up and face homeward and re-entry.

...AND WHILE I WAS OUT

April, May and June, 1965

Politics:

- The first Students for a Democratic Society (SDS) march against the Vietnam war draws 25,000 protestors to Washington D. C.
- Forty men burn their draft cards at the University of California, Berkeley.
- Professors from across the country hold a teach-in in Washington. The event is televised to 122 campuses across the country and covered extensively by the press and mass media.
- The following week, Students for a Democratic Society at the University of California, Berkeley has its first teach-in, drawing over 30,000 people.
- Vietnam protesters march to the draft board in Berkeley, burning nineteen more draft cards and hanging President Johnson in effigy.
- A planned protest at the Pentagon becomes a teach-in and 50,000 thousand leaflets are distributed in and around the building.

Vietnam:

- Nguyen Cao Ky takes over as Prime Minister in South Vietnam. It is the tenth government in Saigon, South Vietnam, in twenty months.

Space:

- Astronaut Ed White makes the first Space Walk as part of the Gemini 4 launch.

International:

- 42,000 Marines are sent to the Dominican Republic by President Johnson to "protect American citizens" and avert an alleged takeover by Communists, preventing "another Cuba."

Culture:

- *My Fair Lady* wins eight Oscars and *Mary Poppins* wins five at the Academy Awards, including Best Actress for Julie Andrews.
- The Astrodome, the first multi-purposed domed sports stadium, opens in Houston, Texas. Officially named the Harris County Domed Stadium, it was the home of the NFL Houston Oilers and the NBL Houston Astros.

PART V

ADIOS AND HELLO?

So, I mustered out, went home, got married, and completed my M.A. in Public Administration. Following my graduation from law school and supported by my loving wife, Ann, we had many great adventures during my long and illustrious career in the Foreign Service. Well, at least, four out of seven of those are true....

I went up to Quito for the last three days in June where we had our medical and dental checkups, feedback sessions, and a Spanish language proficiency test for Peace Corps records. I was finished with all of that by the first of July, but we were not allowed to leave until the 6th, our official termination date. So, we pretty much shopped, partied and drank.

I boarded a plane that took me to Miami on July 6th and arrived at O'Hare in the early morning of July 7th. I was met by the whole contingent: Ann, her mother, her sister, and my parents who had come down from Wisconsin to take me home for the "transition period" we had all read so much about. At this time, there had been much in the press about "reverse culture-shock." A lot of Volunteers experienced culture shock going into countries where the poverty, filth, customs, weather, or other factors were more than they could handle and some, who could not adapt, returned to their homes. But reverse culture shock left one with very few choices about where to go. There was no place to "go." You were home.

For me and so many others, coming home was as unsettling as arriving in the foreign country. The first thing that hit me was the noise: planes, trains and automobiles; Muzak in the elevators; crowds of people talking loudly.... Next, the brightness: everything is illuminated; flashing signs; neon and fluorescent lighting .... Then, all the "stuff": the cars that are new, shiny, bright and going very fast on fast-moving highway systems; homes with a plethora of electronics and appliances for everything; TVs in every house urging you to buy even more.... Finally, the pace – everybody was in a hurry. In Ecuador every time you encountered a person, they would shake hands with you. Each morning when I greeted Suco or the *maestro* we would *"dar la mano,"* (shake hands,) or in the case of a laborer such as the *Maestro* Illescas, *"dar el codo,"* (offer the elbow) to avoid the dirty hand. Here, I noticed that people barely acknowledged each other with more than a "Hi," if that. They were in a hurry, busy, being efficient.

A returning Volunteer quickly learns that most people don't really care about where you've been, what you've done or anything about the country or the people you've visited. Only a few teachers presenting a unit of geography or social studies about the area might have a meaningful inquiry about what you've experienced. An Ecuador Volunteer might get a, "See any headhunters down there?" as some people had heard of the missionary who was killed by the Auca Indian tribes in the Amazon area of the country several years earlier.

Most employers (who the Peace Corps recruiting materials suggested would be eager to hire resourceful, knowledgeable, innovative returning Volunteers) were not particularly interested or impressed with our experience. Some feared that the Volunteer might not fit into rigid, corporate life after the free-wheeling atmosphere of foreign living. Others were wary of the kind of person who had been willing to live on the comparative paltry salary of the Volunteers and that they might not be "driven" enough to work hard to move ahead. Even those entering jobs with the government in Foreign Service or similar positions found themselves mostly unappreciated and placed in low level clerical positions.

I was feeling what I can best describe as "guilt," guilt about having abandoned my friends in South America and not honoring my parting "promise" of going back to Ecuador. I missed "my people." But, after five weeks of back-and-forth trips from Pewaukee, Wisconsin, to Arlington Heights, Illinois; composing our vows; attending a few required counseling sessions with the minister who was to marry us (he had his doubts about me); and the traditional (at the time) bachelor party for me at a local Pewaukee bar, we were married on August 21st. (This was much to the relief of anxious parental units whom I had probably frightened with my own nervousness, reluctance, and doubts.) We had a beautiful wedding. The church was nicely decked out. Ann was a beautiful bride. The bridesmaids were lovely. The reception at the Old Orchard Country Club, complete with a band, was all that one could ask for - picture perfect. We honeymooned with a trip across Lake Michigan, enjoyed meeting with Ann's friends in Michigan, and returned to our two-bedroom apartment on the west side of Madison.

Ann started a job at the Wisconsin Telephone Company, and I started my classes. I discovered how out of practice I was at pouring over large tomes of academic works. I had done my full share of reading in Ecuador but not "exciting" books such as <u>Administrative Decision Making - A Heuristic Model</u> and

Administrative Law and Process. I was in classes with people who had been in the groove of academic life for the last four years, and I was feeling very much out of touch and behind the curve. Our social life consisted of heading back to some of the weekend parties at my old fraternity house - no *trago* but lots of beer. There were at least a few guys I knew from pledge classes that came through before I graduated but brothers from my class were either living elsewhere, married and working new jobs in Madison, or finishing up their third year of law school - not a lot in common, but we did see a few of them from time to time.

On September 25th, a month and four days after our wedding, I was pulled out of class and informed that my father had suffered an abdominal aortal aneurysm while out driving with my mother. By the time we arrived in Pewaukee, he was gone. I was shocked, worried for my mother's condition, and sad that there were no final goodbyes. We hadn't always been very close, but my dad had been very supportive and proud of my efforts in Ecuador, and our relationship had improved. Now he was gone.

We took the required time off for the funeral, and I went back to classes with the triple whammy of: first - re-entry; second - adjusting to married life with a person I hadn't seen in two years except for one hectic month; and third - my father's passing on my mind. I was also asked to pitch in helping my mother deal with the administrative mess created by the fact that my father had died with only a holographic (handwritten) will. A fancy word for that was "intestate," with all the accompanying problems that it entailed. I worked with her and the old attorney who had been my dad's WWI wartime buddy who was a little "over the hill" but, thankfully, had passed the handling of the details to a young associate.

I returned to the grind of going to classes and continued through the year, numbed and marveling at all that was going on around me. Those things included the Watts riots just before our wedding, students marching up and down Bascom Hill on the Madison campus protesting the Vietnam War, people burning draft cards, and announcements about the "War on Poverty." My reaction was, "Give me a break! You want to see poverty? Come along with me to Ecuador, I'll show you what poverty really looks like!" I even said to my Program Advisor, "Why do these anti-war types think they can get anything done marching up and down on a campus? That's not where the legislators are." I was totally unaware of the power the student Free Speech Movement had gained. He seemed to wonder what planet I was from. There were, at the same time, tens of thousands, as well, marching on the Capitol and around the Washington Monument. The Berkley Free Speech Movement had paved the way for all this and more.

It was pretty clear I was thinking with my 1950's mentality, but this was the mid-sixties. Cultural change that used to take a decade was now happening at warp speed. When I left for Ecuador, Elvis and rock & roll were still going strong. Short hair, button down collars and button-down minds were the order of the day. Women often wore hats and gloves to church, meetings, and shopping at the malls, and wouldn't think of going out of the house unless properly attired. The world I returned to, with guys in "long" Beatles haircuts, girls in mini-skirts, and women wearing hair curlers in public, was a shock. "The Day the Music Died" came to mind. Beatlemania and the "British Invasion" were on the airwaves and TV. The largest segment of the population seemed only to care about sports, now neatly marketed and played in new, modern stadiums; the space race ("beat the Russians") and the accompanying technology; getting more "stuff" like modern appliances, modern furniture, modern cars; and getting rid of those "dangerous un-American lefties." The country was being torn in two by rioting, anti-war factions who had no apparent respect for the government or the laws, and the pro-war camps that had no respect for protestors or their views. And neither side was listening to the other.

I coped with all of this by drinking too much. If I learned anything in Ecuador it was how to drink or how <u>not</u> to drink. I was not ready for the "tank" just yet, but weekends of football, basketball, and events on campus provided drinking opportunities to indulge, and I did.

My Public Administration Masters Program came with an internship program, and my assignment was in the Department of Natural Resources for the state of Wisconsin. It was a clerical position logging some statistics for some departmental programs that I don't even recall at this time. What I do remember is my supervisor who had served under two Democratic regimes wandering around bemoaning the fact they had no budget increase and that nothing would happen until another Democratic governor was elected. His attitude, the bureaucracy, and the mundane nature of the work had me down. This was my exposure to working for the government and I wanted to run like hell in the other direction. A bit irrational, perhaps, but I had a major research paper to complete before I could get my degree.

I dedicated myself to the dazzling subject of why and how the city and the state built a major expressway through the middle of Madison and the University Campus. It was a sort of "Who Governs?" approach, and I concluded it was planning commissions. I did my research, interviews and all the rest to make that paper a reality, working through the summer of 1966 when I just ran out of steam. And Ann was running out of patience.

By June of 1966, all our law school buddies had received their degrees and were off to gainful employment at their various firms and posts. Another friend from my fraternity, Ken Miller, who lived near us and with whom we socialized a bit, had just received his PhD. in Pharmacy. He and his wife were off to Connecticut. Ann had taught for two years while I was in Ecuador and now had been at the telephone company for over a year. I got the distinct impression she was ready to "move on up" and let her husband get his oar in the water. Seven years after starting in Madison, it was time to do something. Get a job! I took one more run at the LSAT. I had to balance studies for my degree with studying for the test and I did not do well enough to pass that test. I think I almost didn't care. The thought of three more years of "student poverty," living with brick and board bookcases, bag lunches and all the rest repulsed me. I was tired of the campus protests, the marches, and the simplistic slogans. I was ready to make some money as well. Having completed my course requirements, I made an agreement with my advisor that I would complete my paper by June of 1967.

I didn't know what I wanted to do now that my patriotic bubble had burst. I interviewed insurance companies, the Wisconsin Telephone Company, Caterpillar, and a number of others. I was no real prize as a candidate. One among the insurance companies stood out with their sophisticated (in my mind) approach to estate planning and that was Connecticut General Life Insurance Company, CGLIC. Although I received a couple of other offers, including The Wisconsin Telephone Company, "the missionary" in me said, "Go and save the world from the kind of problems my mother experienced when my father died intestate." That was Connecticut General's main pitch, Estate Planning, and I swallowed it whole. The offer also took us to the Chicago suburb of Lake Bluff, not a bad address to have. The move made Ann very happy. She was back in Illinois and close to home. I got my wingtip shoes, my pinstriped suit and a snap brim hat, and Ann got a new job teaching. We were on our way to suburban living and Ecuador was far behind. Time to "get ahead" or, in my case, catch up.

To telescope time and narrative, CGLIC did not work out very well. They had very good training to enable me to pass the insurance exams. They were a cut above the rest in that sense. The shock to my system when I saw the range of people taking the insurance exam, however, let me know what I was up against. Anyone can be an insurance sales representative if they can pass the test – college and high school grads, or even school drop-outs can do it. The insurance industry is a numbers game. Hire somebody, have them hit up on their friends and relatives for policies and work their network for more. If one has a good network and comes from a connected family or niche you do well. If not, not so much. My network of friends was back in Wisconsin, and CGLIC was looking for a salesman, not a missionary. I didn't have results in any great numbers and was transferred into their Group Sales branch which sold employee insurance programs to corporations. I was sent to places like Cleveland and Indianapolis to call on assigned companies to enroll folks in the plans their companies had purchased, doing the final "pitch and close." But I knew this was not the work for me. I was not happy and my attitude was showing.

I wrote to the Wisconsin Telephone Company recruiter saying in essence, "You were right and I was wrong. I'm interested and hope you are too." They were, and I accepted a position in their Initial Management Development Program in the Commercial and Residential Group. We moved into an apartment in Milwaukee, Wisconsin, but not before I successfully finished the research paper that I had promised my advisor. It was accepted and I got my master's degree in Public Administration. Isn't that nice?

The fit with "Ma Bell" was a good one, and the AT&T Management Training Program was excellent and served me well over the years. Initially we rented and then bought a duplex in Milwaukee, our first house. Ann was able to get a teaching position as well. Almost as soon as we were settled, I got transferred to Madison, and we went first to an apartment and then purchased a ranch home. Ann again got a job teaching there. AT&T was running an effort at job enrichment, a company-wide effort designed to push responsibility down to the lowest level and encourage a team approach to productivity. Right up my alley! I became an advocate for it and, through a friend we had met in Madison, I was recruited to the Harris Bank in Chicago to institute the practice there.

We moved once again, this time to a Highland Park rental home, and soon put a down payment on a home to be built in Hoffman Estates, a suburb thirty miles northwest of Chicago. We moved there in 1971 and made the house a home. We became close friends with the other "pioneers" in the new Centex development, which included the Ray Santini family, with whom I am still in touch.

I sodded the lawn, planted trees and bushes, began a garden, and constructed a built-in bookcase. For the next three years, we painted and wallpapered and did what folks in new houses do - personalized and made upgrades to the contractor's standard installations. I commuted by train from nearby Palatine each day, and Ann taught school in that same suburb until she decided she wanted more out of life. She was eager to follow our friends to an even newer and upgraded part of the development. But after nine moves since our marriage, I was glad to finally have put down roots and was content to stay where we were. Ann became a realtor, bought a Mercedes, worked hard at her profession, and after nine years of marriage, divorced me. She told her sister that she "never loved me."

So, I did muster out, come home, got married and earned my

Master's degree in Public Administration. But I did it in a world that had undergone a major shift in the two years while I was out. Those shifts contained the roots and seeds of things that impacted me and are still shaping our world and our politics today.

EPILOGUE

WHILE I WAS THERE, OIL WAS DISCOVERED IN 1964 IN THE *ORIente* region, the eastern side of Ecuador, through a joint venture by Texaco Petroleum and PetroEcuador. That event was both a curse and a blessing for the country. Before Texaco left the country, it had spilled 17,000,000 gallons of oil into the waterways of the Amazonian region of the country, abandoned hundreds of toxic waste ponds, and opened up 2.5 million acres of forest to colonization. Texaco left, but was replaced by others who continue the devastation to this day, running pipelines through the cloud forests north of Quito. However, the revenues generated from royalties and taxation generated a great deal of development throughout the country and enriched the pockets of the nineteen presidents, military *juntas* and others who have ruled the country in the last fifty-five years, some for only two months at a time. So that feature of Ecuadorian life has not changed.

As I worked on this book in 2015, I was pleased to get a call from Ruben Patiño, my old pal, who wanted to let me know there had been a newspaper article written about the development of the park which would soon be celebrating its 50th anniversary. I actually got some mention as having been involved in its construction. But other than that, my contributions, I suspect, were little known. I sent him some pictures from my files for the occasion. I had hoped to share this memoir with Ruben as he had been a valuable friend, participant, and source for some names and details that my mind could not retrieve. Sadly, he died from a massive cerebral hemorrhage a month before my first draft was completed.

Ruben let me know that both Suco and Padre Arias had gone to their reward. The Padre had continued to be the mover and shaker of La Toma. A review of his obituary showed that he had been the instigator, promoter, and driving force behind a number of developments. They included the construction of the Ovidio Decroly Boys' School and the Gabriella Mistral Girls' School (yes, those of my narrative); collaboration on the start-up of the agricultural cooperative (sounded familiar); an Artisan Center in 1968; a Women's School that had 45 teachers and 504 students; the Night School of Catamayo in 1970; and the installation of an electrical plant that brought substantial power and light to the town. Padre Arias also presided over the Catamayo Cantonization Committee that successfully fought for and won approval in 1981 to become a full-fledged municipality with its own government and officials. And although the article didn't mention it, I'm sure the Padre had something to do with the fact that the Centro Cultural did get its new headquarters that was, of course, surrounded by a wall. In 1982 he was honored as The Outstanding Citizen of Catamayo. Today there is a recreational center and park named after Padre Arias where children and families can enjoy themselves.

You may have wondered, "Did the park in La Toma ever get its water?" Not only did La Toma get water to the park, they now have a water park! There are also several hotels and a number of restaurants, stores and (naturally) several annual festivals. Today La Toma is officially the City of Catamayo with close to 30,000 inhabitants and is the governing body for the Canton of Catamayo. Anything that once looked like the La Toma of my days is long gone.

As for me, after my divorce, I met a wonderful woman at the Harris Bank. Darlene Leesberg was seven years my junior and understood me better than I did myself. After dating for two years, we married in 1976 and spent thirty-five fun, adventure filled years together and were called by one of my conservative banker friends "a couple of hippies in pinstripes." Although not quite apropos since we didn't "do drugs" or live the hippy lifestyle, we were clearly more liberal than most of our banker colleagues. Darlene did much better in the banking world than I, becoming a Vice President of Human Resources. We lived in the same house in Arlington Heights, Illinois, for over twenty-one years.

I stayed with the bank for sixteen years in management development and got involved in behavioral assessment testing and career development, where I found my niche. In 1986, I left the Harris Bank, which had become a subsidiary of the Bank of Montreal. I went into the career development, change management and outplacement field, where I spent the next twenty years as an individual consultant and manager helping others cope with and manage their own transitions.

When our daughter was born in 1984, I decided I had my fill of "*trago*" of any sort and have turned my shot-glass over for the last thirty-seven years. (It took another 12 years before I quit my on-again/off-again smoking habit for good.) My daughter, Kate, has recently made me a grandfather for the first time. Unfortunately, her mother was not present for that, as she passed away from COPD in 2010. We had moved to Mt. Vernon, Ohio, in 2004 to be closer to Dar's family. Kate and her husband, Ian Fraser Ernsberger and daughter, Anastasia Darlene, live there still.

After Darlene's passing, I reconnected with a former girlfriend at a multi-class high school reunion. Katie Anderson was a year behind me, and we started dating the summer after she graduated from high school. (One of our dates was to see *Psycho* soon after it premiered.) We went off to different universities and, as often happens with long-distance relationships, we drifted apart. After that reunion we corresponded, spent some time together, and decided that we could indeed, "pick up where we had left off" so many years before. We got married in 2012; I moved into her home in Atlantic Beach, Florida; and we have spent ten great years together, so far. And, so far, my prostate cancer appears to be under control. We've traveled to many foreign countries together but not to Ecuador.

As Thomas Wolfe wrote, "You can't go home again," and indeed, Ecuador is no longer the country to which I went so many years ago. But they tell me that it is a great place to retire or vacation (with biking, hiking, historical sites and its wonders of nature such as the *Oriente* and the Galapagos.) Perhaps someday soon...

APPENDIX

My case report, as requested by John Smith, that was to be considered for inclusion in a Peace Corps training manual follows:

CASE HISTORY: SCHOOL CONSTRUCTION
by
JERRY REDFIELD PCV

June 1964 Catamayo, Loja, Ecuador

I don't know how much of a case history this will be, or even if it will teach anyone how to win friends and influence people. But it may be of some value to those people who are planning to work in Latin America by showing some of the problems and frustrations that one runs into in this business of, as one Community Development professor put it, "viable nation building."

I am in a town of about 2,500 people that lies in a large valley in the southern Andean mountains of Ecuador. The valley is divided into two distinct halves, the lower half of the valley is green and fertile, covered with sugar cane as far as the eye can see. This cane goes to the sugar mill located in that part of the valley and which gives employment to about 600 people who live here. The upper half of the valley is the town itself. It contains numerous "mom and pop" barbershops, clothing stores, restaurants, and tailor shops fronting the Pan-Am Highway which runs from East to West through the town. Meeting the Pan-Am Highway is another road heading south, along which are more humble restaurants, barbershops, tailor shops, and stores. Farther out there are more little adobe houses. The area in which these houses and the town itself sit is dry and barren with a big "arroyo seco" (dry creek) running through the middle of it.

The school construction program in which I am working is a tri-partite one, with the United States giving a third, the Ecuadorian government giving a another third and the community itself supplying a third in the form of sand, rocks and *minga* (or voluntary) labor. The job of the Peace Corps Volunteer (PCV) in the program is to act as a collaborator among the work force, the local school construction committee, and the Ecuadorian members of Point-Four. The Volunteer can be, if he arrives in the community early enough, instrumental in setting up the local committee. After that his job is to see that the materials keep coming, making sure that they are used with economy, keeping the committee informed of when *mingas* will be needed, and making sure, or trying to make sure, the workers are paid on time. According to the theory, the PCV is free to find other CD projects on which he can work.

I entered the scene here soon after the foundations were poured. The committee was already formed, and I was introduced as a PCV who would work as a collaborator and general watchdog for the construction. The Cuenca Director who introduced me also informed them that I would be looking for other things to do in the community. So, there I was, in a perfect situation: a PCV with a reason for being in the town and introduced as being ready to help in whatever other projects the people were interested in doing. But from there on in, however, it's been an uphill struggle all the way.

My first job was to convince the workers that I wasn't just some Point-Four spy put on the job to make sure that they weren't loafing or robbing materials. This was solved in part, by working as one of the hands for the first three or four weeks. But since there were nine workers, I found that if I stayed on the job, I would be, in effect, robbing someone else's position. So, I ended up by just lending a few tools and mostly supervising. We've been pleased with a maestro who's really organized (a rare thing here) so I found that not much help could be offered in that manner here. In many cases the maestros (the lead carpenters) are anything but organized, and in those cases the PCV can be of immense value in saving time and money. In this case I ended up by going over for about three hours in the morning and three in the afternoon just to see how things were going and to see if any materials were needed. To have just stood there for eight hours a day would no doubt have caused the workers to wonder just what I was there for, if it wasn't to check up on them. At times, when things were going smoothly, I almost asked myself the same question.

This system of a tri-partite program can also cause a few problems as well. Each group is always wondering, "Well whose side are you on anyway?" The answer to that is, and it can be pretty perplexing at times: everyone's! According to the speeches you hear at the inaugurations you'd think it was all one big happy family. But sometimes, during the construction phase you feel as if you were a one-man truce team between two warring camps. The problems arrive for one thing because of the way the program is set up and, more personally, because you as a PCV know the problems that both sides have.

The problems with the program come in the contract itself.

The title says tri-partite but the two governments would, of course, like to see the town contributing more than a third if at all possible. This is usually done by offering to build an extra room or a basketball court if the support of the town is "*suficiente.*" This last is usually in the form of a verbal agreement instead of being placed in the contract itself. Thus, after seven or eight months of fundraising and *mingas,* the local committee is thinking only of fulfilling what is in the contract. But at the same time, it has visions, as in the case of the school here, of an extra room that will be built.

Here the eight rooms stated in the contract had been built and there were many asking why the ninth room, the foundations of which had been poured, hadn't been completed. The priest, who is president of the local committee, told me that they had fulfilled their part of the contract by turning in the designated amount of rocks. There are many times in the program when the PCV has to decide whether to use "we" or "you." In this instance I told him that I believed "we" still had to turn in more rocks if "we" wanted the other room finished. I said, "I'm not sure, but I don't think the contract calls for the construction of that room." By using "we," I was still on "their side" but at the same time pointing out what I knew the program wanted done.

There is only one engineer for all of the 27 or so schools that are going up in the south of Ecuador. As a result, he can't be in all of them or even any one of them very often. Each PVC in this program has to make one trip with the engineer so as to understand his problems a little better. Traveling with him one really begins to see the problems he has and also the great service that this program is doing. He travels day and night, more often than not on roads that seem little more than slightly improved mule trails. It's really refreshing and even inspiring at times, after traveling over such roads for about six hours, to see a building of steel and brick and cement going up in the midst of the adobe houses of some remote village. Here is a building going up which will bring education to the children of this village, and it is a building with ample ventilation and window space. This building, combined with the new books and well-trained teachers which are a part of the program, may give the students a new concept of education and, hopefully, be an incentive for them to go on to further studies.

But I guess we're still building it aren't we? So, let's see what the engineer does when he gets to a site. First of all, he has to check on the construction itself, and comment on or answer some of the problems that exist. One would think that the job of the engineer was done there. But, since the Director of the program doesn't get out to these areas very often, he also has to listen to complaints of lack of payments and materials, go over problems in the contract and generally take chaff for not coming around more often. This done, and maybe a quick bite to eat, and he's on his way again, looking forward to another long drive and more of the same in another town. All this the PCV understands and appreciates. Unfortunately, his town is no different. So, another part of the PCV's job is to make the people understand just what the engineer goes through, and why, although he's the only one that can solve the problems we have, he can't be here every time we need him.

Even if you're aware of the problems involved, the lack of materials can be awfully frustrating to you too. The whole problem lies in the fact that only so much money is allocated to each area every month. This money has to be divided up among all the schools in your area for all the materials needed. Your job (as a PCV) is to see that the materials keep coming, but if there isn't any money on hand, you're in a bind. The committee wants to know where the materials are and so do the workers, especially if they're working on a contract.

Fortunately, or unfortunately, I'm rather close to the Provincial Capitol where the comptroller works. He is one of the "rising middle mass." As a result, this is not his only job. I've made many trips into Loja and spent the whole day looking into offices for him so as to get an order for cement. Sometimes it is there and sometimes it isn't. Even if the order has come in, often your problems still aren't solved.

When we've lacked wooden beams for the roof, I've made many trips to see what was the matter. Talking with the manager of the lumber yard is quite an experience, too. He's either been sick, his truck has broken down, or it's been raining so hard in the *Oriente* that there just hasn't been any way to get the lumber out. But "today everything is fine and tomorrow we can have our lumber." So armed with this heartening information, I return to the workers. Tomorrow comes, and the next day, too. But does the lumber? No! So back I go to see what the trials and tribulations of the manager are today. After a while, so that your word doesn't lose its value, you learn to say that "they say" that it will arrive tomorrow. But since your job is supposed to be to *make* it arrive tomorrow, when the materials don't arrive, they begin to wonder just what value you *do* have. And in some of your more depressing moments, so do you. But then there's the Community Development aspect.

Soon after I got here, I explained to the priest and the secretary of the school construction committee (who is also the president of a local club "for the betterment of Catamayo") that I would also be interested in working on any other projects they think should be done. I explained that I had access to a Cinva-Ram tool with which we could make bricks for latrines or other projects. They thought the machine was a great idea and suggested that it might also be used in the construction of a small community center. They also said that there was a great need for latrines here. (All one needs to do is walk in the streets here to be aware of that!)

Often in those early weeks the "new gringo" was invited out by the local professors. Over a few bottles of the local *"trago,"* something about two steps from rubbing alcohol, we talked over some of their ideas. The latrine idea came up again, and others expressed interest in a library, a playground, and building up a park in the central plaza, which is now nothing more than a dusty square. At first I was rather excited about the whole thing, because everybody seemed to be interested in, and ready for those projects. Then the run around began.

I showed the priest and the secretary of the committee the plans I had for latrines and suggested they could be built very cheaply by using *minga* labor from the town. That was when I first found out something about the town that has been a stumbling block ever since. The idea of a group of townspeople getting together and working together on a project is practically non- existent here. All work is thought of in terms of how much money is necessary to hire a few *peons* to do the work for them. I was informed that there just wasn't any money for such a project. Also, there is not a little resentment toward the Cantonal Capitol in Loja because they have not given much support in the past to projects here according to the local powers that be. As a result, little help is, or was to be expected from them in that quarter.

I kept the latrine idea circulating, and in the meantime went about my work with the school, became the coach of a girls' basketball team from the local girls' school, and also began English classes which have been moderately successful. When it came time to put a wall around the new school, I thought that here was my chance to show what could possibly be done with Cinva-Ram blocks. I asked the PC headquarters to send down the machine.

The night before it arrived the school committee decided to use adobe bricks.

I went ahead anyway and made a few sample bricks using twelve parts of earth to one part of cement. I even talked the secretary in to stopping production on the adobe walls until we saw the results. Well, they liked the results, but they still decided to go ahead with the adobes, because the Cinva-Ram bricks were made of cement and as a result, they would have cost about one and one-half times the cost of the adobes. Again, I got the chat that there just wasn't enough money. However, this time it was modified because they realized that I knew we did have enough. They said that they couldn't spend so much on the wall, because the rest of the money was needed for other projects. These were conveniently left unspecified. It was basically a matter of not wanting to change a method of building that had been used for years.

Not wanting the machine to go to waste, I thought I'd try the *barrio* (neighborhood) approach and see if the people in the *barrio* would like to chip in and build a community latrine. I started my approach by telling them about the need and reasons for building a latrine and finished by telling them how cheaply it could be built. Then I learned something about the town once again. All the families in the *barrios*, except two, are renting their one and two room adobe houses from owners who live on the coast. As a result, they aren't about to spend any of what little money they do make on land they don't own. To them the most important thing is getting enough money to feed their families of five or six or more. If they don't have a latrine, it's not too important. They've gotten along all their lives without one up to now, so why bother?

Checking around I found that the same situation exists in the rest of the town. Catamayo is virtually set in the middle of four of five haciendas. The *hacendados* who are the owners of the fertile lower part of the valley are also the owners of the dry upper part of the valley in which most of the *barrios* lie. The commercial and residential district which forms the town itself was formed by a governmental decree. Thus, the barrios owe more allegiance to the haciendas then they do to the town. They live on, and work on, his land.

Many of the small business owners of the town themselves are renters and have come into Catamayo from other parts. With this combination of factors at work, the feeling of a community spirit is sorely lacking.

It is in this atmosphere that I'm trying to go forward with the Community Development aspect of my work. The priest, who not so incidentally, is a relative of one of the largest land-owning families in the valley, has made such statements in the past as, "The priest is still the soul and leader of the town" and, "In my town, I say what goes." This is generally accepted by the people of the town as the *teniente politico* and the *Junta Parrochial* are considered know-nothing political appointees. To his credit, the priest has been responsible for many projects in the past, and it was almost wholly through his initiative that the school now under construction came to Catamayo. On the other hand, it is very difficult to start any projects of which he is not in favor. The only project to date in which he said he'd give me any support I needed was one which he suggested himself. That was the organization of a 4-H Club here in Catamayo. I obtained the necessary materials and presented them to him. Then I let it ride for a while and later asked him when he wanted to get it started. He told me that, "Once we got the school finished, then we could really get going with the formation of the club."

This phrase has been the story of all the suggested Community Development projects to date. "When we finish the school then..." "When we finish the school then we can get going on a latrine project." "When we finish the school, then we can put a playground next door." "When we finish the school, then we can get an organized sports program going, hold meetings, get a hygiene program going, etc., etc., etc."

So, for now, I'm still plodding along coaching basketball, teaching English, checking and working on the school. As I go about my daily routine, I still keep mentioning some of the projects we have in mind and I still keep getting a lot of favorable responses and the inevitable "When we finish..." So, I keep working, wondering and waiting. And as I finish these "lamentations of Jeremiha" the song on the radio is saying "Quizás, quizás, quizás" ("Perhaps, perhaps, perhaps.")

ACKNOWLEDGEMENTS

I WOULD LIKE TO THANK MY MOTHER FOR SQUIRRELING AWAY my correspondence without which many gaps would appear in my narrative. This book was compiled from my journal and my letters home, which were of utmost help in remembering my time in Ecuador. The letters often contained information that was not included in my journal. (And vice versa!) These missives were especially helpful in recalling the second year of my service in the Peace Corps since (perhaps in one of my many moves) that year's journal was lost. So, thanks to you, Mom. Packrats of the world unite!

None of this work would have occurred without the patience, continued encouragement, and editorial assistance of my wife, Katie Anderson. My thanks to her for hanging in there with me and for the many hours she spent at the keyboard unraveling my fractured prose. Katie's artist's eye was also of great value in the selection, cropping, and placement of the photos in the book; and her creativity provided valuable ideas for the cover design.

My gratitude also goes out to Ruben Patiño, my Ecuadorian pal, for his continued friendship and help in remembering names and participants from the far past which I could not recall. Thanks, as well to his wife, Sandra Torres, who continued to answer questions and inquiries as best she could after Ruben passed away suddenly in October, 2020.

On the professional front, my thanks to Jane Albritton for her editing, helpful comments, and recommendations (one of which spared the reader from the addition of a long "cogent" analysis of the political, social and cultural impacts of the changes I mentioned.) Thanks, also, to Dania Zafar for her book design, layout, and cover expertise. My wife and I appreciate her patience with our nit-picking and willingness to work with us on the many iterations of the content.

Particular thanks to Patricia Wiseman, friend, avid reader, and English teacher, for her detailed proofreading and added editorial suggestions. Her thoroughness and grasp of the English language made me want to include her in the professional ranks.

My appreciation to John Coyne, prolific author and longtime supporter of aspiring Peace Corps authors. His comments, suggestions, and referrals to valuable resources made the creation of this book a much easier task. Thanks, as well, to Marian Haley Biel of the Peace Corps Writers for her valuable instructions and help in bringing this work to the marketplace.

SOURCES

Armentrout, Ana Jane. "The Politics of Experience: Peace Corps Volunteers, Vietnam Veterans, and American Internationalism, 1961-1965." A dissertation submitted in partial satisfaction of the requirements for the degree of Doctor of Philosophy in History in the Graduate Division of the University of California, Berkley. Fall 2012.

Blum, William. *"Killing Hope, U.S. Military and C.I.A. Interventions since World War II."* Common Courage Press. 1995. Chapter *"Ecuador, 1960 to 1963: A Textbook of Dirty Tricks."*

Green, Graham. *"The Quiet American."* Great Britain: William Heinemann Ltd., 1955.

Lederer, William J. & Burdick, Eugene. *"The Ugly American."* New York: The Norton Library., 1958.

Priebus, Jack. *"The Fabulous Peace Corps Booklocker"* www.peacecorpsworldwide.org

The People History. 1963-1964-1965. *thepeoplehistory.com.*

Smitha, Frank. *"World History Timeline."* www.fsmitha.com/1963/1964/1965.htm.

The New York Times. *"The U.S. Economy Now - General Prosperity But Some Persistent Poverty; Economy Booms."* The New York Times, Section E p. 1 May 3,1964.

Thomsen, Moritz. *"Living Poor, A Peace Corps Chronicle."* Seattle & London: University of Washington Press, 1969.

Villazor, Rose Cuison. "*The Immigration Act of 1965 and the Creation of a Modern Diverse America.*" Huffington Post. October 28, 2015.

Wikipedia, The Free Encyclopedia. "1964 In the United States." en.wikipedia.org/wiki/ "1964 In the United States."

Wikipedia, The Free Encyclopedia. "1965 In the United States." *Internet* source.

Wikipedia, The Free Encyclopedia. "The History of Ecuador"/ Incas/Spanish discovery and conquest/Spanish colonial era/Struggle for independence and birth of the republic.

Made in the USA
Las Vegas, NV
29 September 2022

56160109R00167